Not Cool: Europe by Train in a Heatwave

Jules Brown

Published 2020

ISBN 978-1-8380174-9-1

Published by Trust-Me Travel, trustmetravel.com
This book is also available as an ebook

Cover artwork by Chris Hudson Design,
chrishudsondesign.co.uk

For Ripley, who came along in a parallel universe.

Contents

Foreword

IN THE EUROPEAN-wide summer heatwave of July 2019, while sensible people stayed indoors, put their heads in the fridge and watched endless re-runs of *Frozen*, I spent nine days on trains across Europe, visiting nine cities in nine countries.

Why? Good question.

It started off, as most of my ideas do, with a spark of inspiration fuelled by a glass of red wine. Another glass made me think it really was quite a good plan, and by the third glass I had a full itinerary worked up.

If only I'd checked the advance weather forecast, I would have seen that Europe in general, and central Europe in particular, was just about to be engulfed in the mother of all heatwaves. Relentless travel across Europe, jumping from one tin can on rails to another, was going to be decidedly not cool.

But I live in England where a heatwave is what we call it when you have to take your sweater off in July, so it honestly never occurred to me that it would be so hot. That bit's all on me. Definitely my fault.

Everything else that happened? Well that's up to you to decide.

Oh, one more thing. I made this trip before the full force of Brexit and the ravages of Covid and – depending on how far in the future you're reading this – while the planet still had its own ice caps and water supply. So if any of it reads oddly – like, why hasn't he got a mask on, how come they let him into Germany, what's oxygen, that sort of thing – that's why.

Just roll with me as I ride the rails. Like all the best stories, you need to suspend your disbelief.

Back to the Future

Roads? Where we're going we don't need... roads! Dr. Emmett Brown, *Back to the Future.*

CAN YOU REMEMBER what you were doing in the summer of 1980? (I will accept the answer "Busy not being born yet grandad.")

As it happens, I know exactly what I was doing on 11 August 1980 – waiting at Mürren station in the Swiss Alps for the mountain railway and funicular ride down to the lakeside at Interlaken. I was two weeks shy of my eighteenth birthday and had just finished a three-week stint at an international youth workcamp high in the Alps, where twenty of us from a dozen different countries stayed in a creaking wooden chalet straight out of *The Sound of Music.*

By day we dug footpaths between precariously sited mountain villages overlooked by the pointy summit of the Schilthorn; if there were lonely goatherds, we didn't see any, though I dare say we crushed a fair bit of *edelweiss* under foot. By night we cooked crisp apple *strudels* and *schnitzel* with noodles, flirted hopelessly with each other and learned random words in many and varied languages. For some unaccountable reason I can still say "Can you pass me the soap dish" in Dutch. At least, that's what they told me it meant.

We went to a village festival where the local DJ (almost certainly just one of the farmers in a spangly T-shirt) played Phil Collins' 'In the Air Tonight' on permanent loop and everyone got drunk on barn-distilled schnapps. At dawn the next morning we were tasked with holding ropes, untying knots and helping to launch hot-air balloons into the Alps, which on reflection doesn't seem like a sensible job to entrust to horny, hungover seventeen-year-olds.

The footpath work was hard and repetitive – hacking out rocks with pick and shovel, building steps and hauling gravel – but every now and again the team leader let someone push the button that set off the dynamite under obstructive rocks. Actual dynamite, in the hands of teenagers. I wouldn't trust my own teenagers to look after a hamster, yet we were allowed – encouraged – to blow up bits of Switzerland. There's alpine landscape out there that I personally fashioned; they should probably make me a citizen.

After three weeks of digging, dynamite and drinking (though never all three at the same time – that would just be asking for trouble) it was time to leave, which is why I found myself waiting at Mürren station in August several decades ago.

I have absolutely no memories of that day, but the reason I know I was there is because of a handwritten entry in my InterRail pass, which I've kept in a shoebox for years alongside old passports and other travel mementoes. The scheme is still going strong and the concept is simple – you pay a fixed amount and get to travel around Europe by train for free, anywhere you like, for up to a month. It's been a celebrated rite of passage since 1972 and InterRail – Eurail for non-Europeans – has done more to open up travel in Europe for young people than any other initiative you can think of.

These days, you might be able to fly directly and cheaply to Spanish beaches, Italian cities and Greek islands, but that way you're cocooned in a bubble from start to finish. You drink, party, fall over and sleep in late in your chosen resort and then return home, bubble intact, mind possibly altered by illegal Class A drugs but otherwise unbroadened.

Travel by train and the bubble bursts. You see how France is connected to Germany is connected to Austria is connected to Italy in a giant geography lesson ("It's fun kids, really!"). You cross your own continent in real time. You literally put yourself on the map. You also drink, party, fall over and sleep in late – and sometimes you do all of those things on the same train – but when you get back, something in you has changed. Turns out, there are people in all those in-between countries doing things in different ways, living lives that diverge from yours in all sorts of fascinating ways. Maybe the world didn't get any bigger, but it sure just got a whole lot more interesting than spending a week with a load of wasted Brits in Benidorm (which you can also get to by train, by the way, just in case the destination is a deal-breaker).

My own rail trip that distant summer took me through ten countries in four weeks, with first visits for me to Switzerland, Austria, Belgium, the Netherlands and Denmark. Naturally, I dipped my toes in Lake Geneva, chortled at the Mannekin Pis in Brussels, walked wide-eyed around Amsterdam's Red Light district and toured the Carlsberg factory in Copenhagen. It would have been rude not to. I also waited patiently on platforms, slept fitfully on trains, washed patchily in stations, wrestled a bulky backpack through various European capital cities, and learned more about life in a few weeks than I had in the last few years of school. On, I might add, the low, low sum of five quid a day, which grand amount paid for a hostel bed, a picnic lunch, a cheap evening meal and even a beer or two along the way.

Five pounds in 1980 is the equivalent today of about twenty-two pounds, so times have definitely changed. You'd struggle to pay for a night's hostel accommodation alone with twenty-two pounds in most big European cities, so it seems that – despite the eye-rolling – I may actually have a point when I bang on to my teenagers about how things were better in the old days.

The other thing that occurs to me is how relaxed – outwardly at least – my parents were about my first European train tour.

I wasn't yet eighteen. Technically I suppose they could have objected when I came home and said "Guess what I'm doing this summer? Yes, there'll be dynamite, beer and girls," but as far as I remember they were entirely encouraging and drove me to Huddersfield station to wave me off. This seems remarkably trusting, not just in me but in the world, given that – before cell phones, email and internet – they wouldn't really hear from me for the next seven weeks. I'm sure I promised to send a postcard or two, but that was hardly real-time reassurance that everything was all right. They would only know I was safe when I got back off the train again in England or they took a call from whichever embassy I had sought refuge in when I lost my passport and ran out of money.

Were they at all worried as they stood on the platform? I know I'll be freaking out about the endless permutations of travel danger when I send my own children off around the world, despite the secret location and data tracking I've installed on their phones and the chips I had inserted into their temples when they were babies.

My parents though, I'm not so sure. Dad at least wouldn't have had a leg to stand on had he tried to raise any objections. He'd spent years telling me about his adventures. At seventeen, Dad had cycled from Cambridge to France and back – camping out under the stars in a Europe recently torn apart by war. A few years later he did his National Service in the Far East, and then volunteered in a refugee camp in Germany. He drove Mum to Barcelona in 1958 for their honeymoon – when Barcelona was a dodgy port city with attitude and not a designer lifestyle destination – and two years later got a teaching job in Ghana, West Africa. In total, he worked in forty-seven different countries, doing glamorous gigs in the South Seas and West Indies; he undertook hot and dusty tours of East Africa and spent weeks at a time at provincial universities in million-strong cities you've never even heard of in Northern China. Together with mum, he travelled overland from India to Nepal, flew around Mount Everest, gazed upon Machu Picchu, walked on the Great

My first press trip – a week's holiday, all expenses paid, nothing too much trouble – was hosted by the affable Swedish Tourist Board and it took place entirely on a train. There's a thirteen-hundred-kilometre-long Swedish railway line, the Inlandsbanan, that they wanted to promote and they calculated, quite correctly, that if they wined and dined a young, broke backpacker he would write favourable things about the route in his *Rough Guide to Scandinavia*. I'll never know if they think they got their money's worth – probably not, given the price of Swedish beer and the instruction to me to "Drink as much as you like, we're paying." But I do know that the experience of travelling by train through the whole of central Sweden was a formative one. I had a window seat on the country, from the southern lakes to the Arctic Circle, and was introduced to a slow-paced Sweden that otherwise would have been hidden from me. Elk and reindeer encroached upon the line and the train had to stop occasionally to let them clear the tracks. On other occasions that the train called a halt with no station in sight, it was usually because the guard wanted to point out a beaver damming a nearby stream or to let people off to swim in a lake or pick wild berries. At the Arctic Circle, the Inlandsbanan stopped again and we all piled out for souvenir photographs, with one foot planted either side of the painted white rocks that represented the line. Being a snarky, ungrateful little so-and-so, I felt compelled to point out in the Rough Guide that this was a waste of everyone's time since the Arctic Circle is not fixed and shifts a few metres each year towards the North Pole. The Swedish Tourist Board was too good-mannered ever to mention it and, the more I travelled, I learned that life was better all round if I was less cynical and more positive, so perhaps they did get a reward on their investment after all.

After that, I travelled overland by train to Narvik in the far north of Norway, across the Alps to Barcelona and as far south as the Algarve in Portugal, collecting material for guidebooks that were largely aimed at people like me – interested in what wasn't yet called "slow travel," involving a human-scale appreciation of landscape and culture, delighted by byways and backwaters, happy to see what was on the way. Moving around by train forced you to take stock, look out of the window and watch the world go by – and in doing so, you learned more about how each country worked than you realised.

Take Italy, for example. I once shipped a computer overland by train to Italy. I know, what was I thinking? I say computer. I actually mean Amstrad word processor, which was like a very heavy and bulky PC the size of a small desk that didn't do any personal computing at all, or in fact do anything useful except write text. Which I could have done in a notebook. "It'll be there in three days," they said in London. I was sceptical. It takes three days just to buy a stamp in Italy. But amazingly, it was there in three days, waiting for collection at a Sicilian train station. It then took another three months to extract my own property from the station, after about a hundred visits conducted in rudimentary Italian and accompanied by exasperated shouting (me) and exaggerated shoulder-shrugging, sighing and eyebrow-raising

17

(everyone in officialdom, plus random passing Sicilian strangers who never like to pass up on a good argument). There were also irregular payments of "fees," endless paper-stamping and the acquisition of an Italian tax code, borrowed from a woman in the local tourist office who I barely knew at all – which, incidentally, seemed like an entirely normal solution to her. I had the use of the computer for about three weeks, before I had to return it and me to the UK, also by train. The entire Sicily guide that I had been commissioned to write was contained in the notebooks that I should have brought with me in the first place.

Since then I've departed Grand Central in New York, crossed the Bridge over the River Kwai, traversed New Zealand, travelled through the Pyrenees and the Scottish Highlands, sped into Hong Kong and rattled from Singapore to Malaysia – and each of these rail journeys began with the same thrill of anticipation as the train pulled slowly away and the country started to unfurl. While it's fanciful, I like to imagine that I sat in those bouncy second-class European carriages all that time ago, face pressed to a train window, lost in thought, dreaming of the future, clanking through a wider world that was to become my back yard, my canvas, my career in the decades that stretched ahead.

Too much? Maybe. But it makes me think. Train travel has been a big part of my personal and professional life, but I've never repeated a similar trip. Hundreds and hundreds of trains in countries right across the world, yes. But a big old multi-country European train extravaganza? Well no, and why not?

So I sit around a map of Europe late one spring and come up with a plan for a nine-day train ride through as many cities and countries as possible. Nine days, because that's the time I have available later in the summer; and as many cities and countries as possible, because I do like a pointless challenge. I decide to establish some ground rules too, because what's a pointless challenge without rules?

Rule 1 – spend only one night in each place because, for this trip, the travel by train will be the point of my journey. I'm looking forward to seeing Europe roll by through a train window, daydreaming about life and travel and relaxing into that half-asleep-half-awake mode that descends upon you as the train wheels clatter through waving fields of wheat studded with poppies.

Rule 2 – no chasing around European capital cities ticking off famous sights and iconic attractions. What would be the point? Instead, I will make a virtue of my limited time and choose just one thing to do – a walk, an offbeat sight, a random attraction – that will still make me feel like I have experienced something real in that particular city.

I stop at two rules, partly because I can't think of more but mostly because when I look at the potential itinerary I realise it isn't going to be a simple matter of buying a railpass and jumping on trains when I feel like it.

To get the most bang for my buck – the largest number of destinations in the shortest time possible – I settle on the following route: from Berlin to Prague, Vienna, Bratislava, Ljubljana,

Zagreb, Liechtenstein, Zürich and Milan. It makes the most of proximate capitals and countries, includes one overnight sleeper train (Zagreb to Zürich); two of the greatest of all European rail journeys (the Semmering Railway between Vienna and Graz, and over the Bernina Pass from Switzerland to Italy); and two side trips to tick off Slovakia and Liechtenstein. It also has novelty on its side. There are quite a few places on that list I've never been to (Berlin, Ljubljana, Zagreb) and some others (Vienna, Zürich) that I visited long ago but really don't remember. If I'm being honest, there are also one or two that I'd be hard-pushed to place on a map — Bratislava, Ljubljana, higher, lower?

You could — just about — still do a trip like this by just turning up with a railpass and catching each train on the day. But times have changed since the early days of InterRail. Most international routes now require advance reservations, and I haven't got time to mess around waiting for slower, local trains. Places to go, cities to visit, pointless itineraries to follow. I've got nine days. I need it organised, booked and confirmed, so I set to work.

That lasts about ten minutes before I close down every tab on the computer and do some deep breathing.

What you find out quite quickly is that every European country has at least one train operator, often more, each with their own website and ticketing system. I'm visiting nine different countries. There's no one place you can go to buy all the tickets you need. It also goes without saying that I know nothing about the train operators running the route between Zagreb and

Zürich, or which side of the carriage to sit on for the best views over the Bernina Pass between Switzerland and Italy. How do you get to Liechtenstein by train when Liechtenstein doesn't have any trains? I have no idea. Can you reserve a seat on a train in the Czech Republic? Can I get an e-ticket on an app to show a train guard in Slovenia? Respectively, who knows and feck knows.

However, I'll tell you who knows, and you'll thank me for this later. An Englishman called Mark Smith knows, who writes under the name The Man in Seat 61. If you haven't heard of him already, Google him; I promise that he will change your travelling life.

The Man in Seat 61 knows everything about trains. He's the reason I am about to arrange tickets for all the trains I want to travel on without suffering a nervous breakdown. His website – a creative obsession really rather than a thing of coding, bytes and updates – is a work of frighteningly organised and highly informative genius. Pick a train route – any route, anywhere in the world – and The Man in Seat 61 tells you how to book it at the cheapest possible price. It's startlingly comprehensive – Armenia to Zimbabwe – and diverting in the extreme, so that you start off looking up, say, Berlin to Prague and end up down the rabbit-hole on the Trans-Siberian wondering how many days' stopover you really need in Ulan Bator (The Man says three).

The Man in Seat 61 does that to you. He makes it easy to arrange train trips, and shows you how it's done, step by step, but what he really does is package dreams. Here's the world, he says. You don't have to fly. Take the train. It's romantic. It's simple, it's straightforward, and it's better for the planet.

With the help of the wonderful Seat 61 website, I book all the tickets and reserve all the seats, with five different train companies, and store the tickets on three separate apps and back them up on eleven different print-outs. I make all the timetables available both online and offline on two more apps, and the only thing that I don't organise in advance is the train from Ljubljana to Zagreb because if you buy the ticket at the station the day before you travel it's half price and only costs nine euros. And I know this because – of course – The Man tells me.

So it's all done and the trip is on, and because it's been so brilliantly organised – why thank you – I am tempted to ask, what could possibly go wrong?

Granted, catching many, many trains in many, many different countries in such a short space of time can only be amusing at my expense, as I fail to understand the German for "The train to Prague now leaves from platform two" and end up in Bucharest instead. But let's assume that all my plans go swimmingly. I will see you in nine days' time, when my second big European train adventure – forty years after the first – comes to an end following a record-quick romp through nine cities and nine countries. I'm looking forward to seeing Europe at speed, sampling some snapshot experiences and riding the rails across the continent's most dramatic landscapes. I'll report back, don't worry, you won't have to do anything.

I've made a few more advance plans, just to keep things simple while I'm on the move. You will have noticed a rather wholehearted reliance on reservations, apps, e-tickets and printed back-ups. In theory this means I shouldn't have to check departures and timetables, so I won't be needing a big red *European Rail Timetable*. Astoundingly, it still exists – now an independent guide after Thomas Cook stopped publishing it in 2013, and still very much the place to find out, for example, about the slow train from Sofia to Thessaloniki. But I'm going to say that I'm sorted for timetables and thank them very much for their service – and if I end up by mistake on the overnight Bulgaria-to-Greece sleeper then I will only have myself to blame.

As predicted, budget accommodation – let alone everything else – costs rather more than a fiver a night in Europe now. A quick Google search tells me that Zürich is the most expensive European city to visit and that Milan is the priciest place in Italy; I can't imagine that five pounds goes far in Berlin and Vienna either. However, I am no longer an impoverished student and if I don't spend my money it'll only be frittered away by my children once they sign the papers and bung me in a home.

The good news is that there's a lot more choice than there was when I first started travelling. I don't just have to stay in the only cheap place in town. Hostels have gone and got posh – someone once coined the word "poshtel," forgive them for they know not what they do – while there are decent if unexciting budget hotels everywhere. All I ask is that I get my own bathroom and that I don't have to tramp around strange cities on arrival looking for a

Berlin

No. Even now I can't altogether believe that any of this really happened.
Christopher Isherwood, *Goodbye to Berlin.*

BERLIN, I AM led to believe by numerous books and websites, has a temperate climate "characterised by moderately warm summers." Hell, Hades, blazes, a monkey's bum, an oven, a Carolina Reaper chilli and a dingo's sphincter, on the other hand, are all generally considered to be extremely hot, and it has honestly never occurred to me to add "German capital" to that list of similes until I step off the plane at Berlin Schönefeld Airport.

It's hot in a face-searing, bone-sapping, migraine-inducing way that they definitely don't warn you about before they open the plane door – "Welcome to Berlin where the local temperature is WHAAAAAT the …" There's a blast of scorching air as I emerge on to the plane steps and passengers leave strips of skin on the metal handrail as they grasp it for support. The short walk to the terminal building is a sort of German hot-coal initiation ceremony, only with a hundred metres of tarmac and concrete and no cooling off the feet in a palm-fringed sea. The local news report will doubtless lead with the story that flights were disrupted at Schönefeld Airport today when planes literally melted on landing.

"Yes Hans, that's correct, the puddle you can see on the runway is in fact Easyjet flight EJ357, and now back to the studio."

It's not even the hottest day of the year. That was a couple of weeks earlier, when the city hit a record thirty-nine degrees Celsius (over a hundred Fahrenheit in old money), though when you're this far up a dingo's sphincter what's a couple of degrees between friends? Thirty-nine is not "moderately warm." You wash a pair of soiled jeans at thirty-nine to get rid of the stubborn stains after that night in the club when you... anyway, doesn't matter. Thirty-nine is insanely hot for Europe. Thirty-nine is beyond the boiling point of isoprene, phosgene, pentene, ethyl bromide and trichlorofluoromethane and, while I don't know what any of those things are, I do know it's not a good idea to boil them. Thirty-nine means I've already got sunburned kneecaps and I'm thinking the "thin long-sleeved fleece" from the packing list is probably a bit *de trop*.

Still, here I am and off we go. The first train on the first day of my Big Summer Train Trip – I've decided it warrants capital letters – is the half-hourly regional express from Schönefeld Airport to Berlin city centre. In the next nine days, I'm going to travel almost three thousand kilometres by train across central Europe as I trace the Danube, penetrate the Balkans and traverse the Alps, and it all starts with the short thirty-minute ride to Berlin's main station, the Hauptbahnhof.

Sadly, I'm going to have no need of the one useful phrase in German that was drilled into us in Mr Hargreaves' class in school

– namely, *Wo ist der bushaltestelle?* (Where is the bus stop?). Instead, I simply follow the handy sign from the airport that says "Trains," so nuts to Mr Hargreaves. I buy a ticket from the automatic machine in the concourse, see from the departure board that the Berlin train is about to leave, sprint down the tunnel, follow the signs and run up a steep flight of steps to the platform. I say all that like it's easy – sprint, run, up the steps. Picture a red-faced, glistening man who looks like he's just eaten a vindaloo and dipped himself in lard, wading in slow-motion through treacle-like air while carrying a bag full of clothes more suited to a winter ski holiday. Imagine, if you will, a heavy-breathing, rucksack-carrying gent moving with all the sprightly ease of a prison escapee hobbled by ankle chains and negotiating a muddy field. Yep, that's me.

The train's idling, engine running, doors open, so I clamber on, find a seat and stow the backpack. I'm ten minutes out of the airport and already wringing wet – so much so that I don't want to lean back against the seat because of that terrible, clingy feel of sweaty shirt against skin. Doors close, the train pulls off on time and I look out of the window as we trundle through Berlin's suburbs on a piercingly bright summer's day, clackety-clacking through stations with offputtingly long compound names.

It's taken four months of meticulous planning to get to this point. I've taken trains all over the world, from Norway to New Zealand and Sicily to China – not those actual routes, you understand – and I take my travel prep seriously. There's nothing I like better than devising train journeys, plotting routes and chasing down the information I need to make the trip a success. Four months of reading, Googling, writing and printing. Sixteen weeks of checking train timetables, noting down departure times and confirming connections. One hundred and twelve days of filling in spreadsheets, downloading apps and making seat reservations. Two thousand six hundred and eighty-eight hours of learning the words "train station" in a variety of European languages, not all of them with vowels or consonants in the expected places.

It goes without saying that I'm on the wrong train.

To be fair to me – and I think you must try, despite the clear temptation to laugh your head off – it's not at all apparent at any point that I've made a mistake. Stations come and go, all prefixed with the word Berlin, so we pass through Berlin Ostkreuz, Berlin Ostbahnhof, Berlin NichtThisWay and Berlin DummkopfIdiot, though I'm not really paying much attention and may have misread a couple of them. And I'm not really paying much attention because I followed the signs to the correct platform. As far as I'm concerned, I'm on the train to Berlin from the airport which terminates at Berlin Hauptbahnhof and so I don't need to worry about it because the train will just stop when it gets there.

Except, after about forty minutes, just as the train is leaving another random suburban station – Berlin ScheißeVerdammt as I recall – there's an announcement that says, "Next station, Berlin Schönefeld Airport."

Wait. What?

I look around at the other people in the carriage, none of whom seem to be panicking or hyperventilating, and all of whom appear quite clearly to be heading to an airport, with their labelled luggage, passport holders and care-free demeanour. I sit tight and say nothing as the train passes back through Berlin DummkopfIdiot, Berlin NichtThisWay, Berlin Ostbahnhof and Berlin Ostkreuz, until it terminates half an hour later at Berlin Flughafen Schönefeld, where delighted holidaymakers pour off the train and into the airport terminal.

I grab my backpack, stand on the platform and try and look as if the hour and a half's round-trip back to where I started was entirely the beginning that I had in mind for my trans-European train extravaganza. Can't be too careful, just checking, belt and braces and all that. Now I know that's definitely *not* the train, it's time to get cracking, best foot forward, onwards and upwards. I cross the platform to the other track where the actual train to Berlin Hauptbahnhof is just about to depart, jump on, find a seat and stow the backpack. This time we bypass Berlin NichtThisWay and Berlin DummkopfIdiot in favour of Berlin Alexanderplatz and Berlin Friedrichstraße – well done driver, I knew you could do it – and pull into the main station roughly two hours later than planned.

I have since discovered that there is an excellent German phrase, *Ich verstehe nur Bahnhof,* whose literal translation is "I only understand train station." Germans use it when they don't understand something – rather like we might say "It's all Greek to me" – and I can't think of a better opportunity to try it out. I still have no idea what happened, or how it was that the train went in an entire circle without me noticing – in fact, *Ich verstehe nur Bahnhof* – but we are where we are (Berlin, I think) and will say no more about it. Stop sniggering at the back there.

Berlin Hauptbahnhof is one of those modern railway stations that badly wants to be an airport, with its elevated terraces, shopping concourses, ersatz street-food kiosks and café zones. If only they had some of those plane things and a runway, but they're stuck with the boring trains. The tracks are all tucked away underground – "All right, if we have to have the trains, they're going right down there, where no one can see them" – and I rise on zig-zag escalators into a vast, soaring, glass-roofed hall. It's undeniably impressive and, if I'm honest, all a little disappointing for the adventurous traveller.

Time was, you got off a train in a major European city and emerged into a grimy, smoke-filled concourse where tramps were foraging in bins and gangs of urchins were harassing fresh-faced American students carrying towering backpacks. Out on the street, you'd be thrown straight into the Red Light district and introduced to several unkempt, hollow-faced people with grasping hands eager to make your acquaintance. You'd run the gauntlet – drugs? why how kind, no, I'm sure she's lovely, etc – try to look like you knew where you were going and never, under any circumstances, book into any of the hotels within eyesight of the station. These were called things like Hotel Gunshot or Organ Harvest Gardens and rarely troubled the local tourist board's star-rating system. There was a place I remember around the back of the Rossio station in central Lisbon, the rather gritty Pension Iris, whose "en-suite twin room" indeed had both shower and toilet, but plumbed bang into the centre of the room and separated from the beds by a pull-round shower curtain. The proprietor maintained a twenty-four-hour reception by the simple expedient of sleeping under his desk on a soiled mattress, baseball bat to hand. When you rolled in at two am, unsteady on your feet after a night of Portuguese hospitality, he'd pop his head up, check you were a guest and not someone who needed a tap on the bonce with a baseball bat, and be fast asleep again by the time you hit the stairs. In the dive bar next door, a down-at-heel businessman in a shabby suit once beckoned me over, reached into his pocket (no, not what you're thinking) and proudly showed me his gun.

Ah happy days. But as I say, long gone in most of Europe and especially around Berlin's sparkling, glass-fronted Hauptbahnhof, where the worst that's going to happen to you is a squirt of designer perfume in the eye from an over-keen shop assistant.

I'm still on a budget though, so nothing too fancy for accommodation, which in Berlin means the Hotel Mitte Campanile, ten minutes' walk from the station down a busy but unthreatening boulevard. They have managed to acquire a cunning three and a half stars, so well done to them, and I submit the room to my usual quick hotel check – namely, are there any little shampoo bottles to nick (yes), do the curtains close properly (yes) and are there any English-language channels on the TV (yes). That's three stars right there in my book, and when I discover that there are also tea- and coffee-making facilities in the room – any right-thinking British traveller is currently sharing my unexpected joy – I think that explains the mysterious extra half a star rating.

As for climate control, I can have the air-conditioning on, which makes a noise that sounds like a washing machine filled with rocks, or I can turn it off and open the window, in which case the temperature rises dangerously close to the levels where little-known chemicals start to boil. In either scenario I'm not going to get a wink of sleep, but I'll worry about that later.

I dump my bags, bounce on the bed a bit and consider my options.

On one hand, my time in Berlin has just been reduced by two hours because – well, no need to go over that again. On the other hand, this is not a sightseeing tour in the usual sense. I don't have to chase down sights in a great orgy of list-ticking, and I can't possibly see all that Berlin has to offer in any case. I'll be gone by seven o'clock tomorrow morning. It's not Berlin or bust. This is a case of Berlin "in and out" – no roll call of famous sights and attractions, but instead a quirky experience or two that shows me the city in a particular light, and then back on to the train (hopefully the right one).

All that being said, this is my first time in Berlin. Of course I'm going to see the Brandenburg Gate, Checkpoint Charlie and the Berlin Wall. Did you think I was just going to visit the Hanf Museum – they say "Germany's only hemp museum"; I say, "No kidding" – and have done with it? Rules, my friends, are made to be broken, especially ones you devised yourself late one evening on the wrong side of three glasses of Rioja.

Until now, Berlin has never been on my radar. I haven't been to Germany since I InterRailed around Europe forty years ago and, while I'm sure it has many fine points, I have never been minded to investigate further. Partly, I'm sure, this is because my soul is in the south – Italy, Greece, Spain, Portugal – where life is colourful, loud and outwardly chaotic; where drivers park on green traffic lights to have a chat with a passer-by; where opening hours, government statements and police notices are more in the way of suggested guidelines than orders and regulations; where two people in a market having a friendly conversation about fish sound as if they have grievously insulted each other's mother and are about to come to blows. The characteristics I look for in a nation are unruliness, irregularity, waywardness, *brio* and *vida loca* – and unless I've been sorely misled by national stereotypes, always a possibility I admit, then Germany is not the place to find them.

But if you're going to start a trans-European rail journey, you don't want to start it in Athens, Lisbon or Madrid, because each is a long way from anywhere and there's only one straight line to go in before you reach somewhere else. Berlin, though, is perfect. It's at the centre of a rail network that reaches in all compass directions – within a day's travel you can be in one of a dozen different countries. So Berlin it is, and I have the rest of the day to chalk off some famous sights just in case it's another forty years before I return.

A quick fifteen-minute walk from the hotel puts me outside the Reichstag – the German parliament building – which rises up above the River Spree. Opened in 1894, with a grand façade inspired by Philadelphia's Memorial Hall and topped by a glass dome, few parliament buildings have been so put upon in such a short time. It was the seat of government only until 1933, when it caught fire in mysterious circumstances, allowing the Nazis to suspend its powers; then it was bombed and ruined during the Second World War, and abandoned when the West German government was established later in Bonn. It's only been the home of the German parliament again since 1999, after being famously wrapped in fabric by artist Christo and then given a fancy restoration by Norman Foster.

You have to register and book in advance to climb to the roof terrace and dome – no, sadly, I'm not that organised – so I take a quick peek at the Neoclassical exterior and then stroll on another five minutes to the Brandenburg Gate, one of the historic, monumental entrances to the city and symbol of German unification.

I don't often advertise it, but I have a history degree from a world-renowned British university. Dreaming spires, Inspector Morse, all that. I know, hard to believe. In fact, one of my colleagues, once informed of the fact, said "Really?" rather too quickly. But it is the case that I spent three years in some of England's most beautiful library buildings reading books by

35

notable historians – I could have gone to lectures by notable historians but that would have meant getting out of bed – and wrote barely adequate essays about esoteric topics, all of which I forgot the minute I left university. I can tell you a few things about the Vikings, Robert Peel's Second Ministry or the medieval strip-farming system, but if I'm honest the most useful thing I learned was how to employ that extremely useful phrase "Not my period I'm afraid," beloved of historians everywhere.

This is by way of saying that, despite my education – in actual European history – shamefully, I know very little about German history and next to nothing about contemporary German politics. Not my period I'm afraid. This, then, is not the book for a nuanced discussion about the role the Brandenburg Gate has played in different periods of German history. And whatever I do tell you, you're going to be thinking, "Yeah, sounds plausible, but this is the guy that caught the wrong train from the airport."

Equally, I feel I need to do better than the travel bloggers and writers who just point out the Brandenburg Gate as an awesome and cool must-see sight and then move you on to the next Instagram stop. If travel writing has any use – let's just pretend – then it's as much about insight as it is inspiration, and it should provide at least some context, both for the writer and the reader. Standing under one of Europe's most resonant landmarks, just an hour or so after getting off the train, is about more than just bucket-list-ticking for me.

If you're European, the Brandenburg Gate is where your modern continent was forged. Built at the end of the eighteenth century, its soaring, fluted columns and chariot-topped pediment are based on the ancient gateway to the Acropolis in Athens. Napoleon marched through, the Nazis co-opted it in their show parades, and presidents Kennedy, Reagan, Clinton and Obama all spoke here in the name of freedom. The Gate survived the Second World War and then stood sentry at the neighbouring Berlin Wall until that fell in 1989; a year later, the flag of a reunified Germany was raised over the Gate. It's a scene I watched on TV – history being made – and while standing at the Brandenburg Gate now brings back certain personal memories, it also provokes a few 'what ifs'. History could have turned out very differently, in 1945 or even 1989. There was no guarantee that liberty would prevail so that travel writers could stand under the Brandenburg Gate today and tell you how cool and awesome it is.

The problem with reducing everything to ticks on a list and images on a feed is made doubly apparent another few minutes' walk down the road from the Brandenburg Gate. I'm walking on to Checkpoint Charlie and following the map on my phone when I see a plaza of dark grey concrete slabs ahead of me. It's a difficult scene to describe. Think of rectangular shapes, each the same length (two-and-a-half metres) and width (one metre) but of varying heights from twenty centimetres to almost five metres high. Then think of precisely two thousand seven hundred and eleven of them, arranged in a huge grid across a sloping square, so that the concrete slabs run in undulating rows, alleys and canyons, forming a maze-like landscape through which you can wander at will.

My phone mapping tells me this is the Memorial to the Murdered Jews of Europe, whose title couldn't be clearer about the nature of the site. It's Germany's main memorial to those Jews killed in the Holocaust, sited deliberately close not only to the Brandenburg Gate but also to the Chancellory and air-raid bunker complex from where Hitler ran his murderous war. The visual references and symbolism – the rows of tomb-like slabs, the disorienting descent into ghetto-like alleys, the gradual loss of daylight in the deepest depths – can't be lost on anyone, even those who stumble upon the memorial on their iPhone, as I have.

Yet lost they seemingly are, with those same iPhones being used for selfies and videos by people clambering up on the pillars and dangling their legs off the edge. I walk through the dark concrete trenches, while young adults leap out at each other from behind angular walls and others pose astride the coffin-like slabs and flash thumbs-up at their girlfriends. There are squeals and laughs, and cold drinks downed on concrete rectangles that stand for millions of murders. But hey, it's an amazing sight guys and check out my Instagram.

I don't think I'm virtue-signalling here. I'm not unusually empathetic and I'm pretty sure I've done and said things in various locations around the world that are culturally insensitive. I don't understand every nuance of religion or social order, and I flaunt my freedoms – to travel, to write, to talk openly – without often checking my privilege. I could even make a half-hearted argument that having the freedom to act in this way at such a site is what a war was fought for. But I stand among the slabs of a brutal memorial, amid people who don't know and don't care what it represents, and all I can think is: feckin' eejits.

I move on to Checkpoint Charlie, another twenty minutes across town on foot. The name resonates across the decades – the most famous crossing between the old East and West Berlin and yet another symbol in a city full of them. Cold War crossing-point C (for Charlie) in the Berlin Wall, the checkpoint looms large in history, films and spy novels – US and Soviet tanks faced off across it in 1961, while it was immortalised in John le Carré's *The Spy Who Came in From the Cold*. Spooks, diplomats and officials mingled and sparred at this infamous crossing point of the Berlin Wall, while others suffered darker fates. Eighteen-year-old East German Peter Fechter, for example, was shot trying to escape from east to west and bled to death at the crossing while tangled in barbed wire. The checkpoint stood until the fall of the Wall, after which it became an out-and-out tourist site, now attracting millions of visitors a year.

Despite sporadic attempts to develop the site sensitively it's basically a traffic-swamped zoo, with a fake US Army Checkpoint and guard house announcing, "You are leaving the American sector." There's McDonald's and KFC, a row of tourist-tat gift shops and milling crowds of people wandering about going "Is this it? Really?" It's hard to think about the history – and certainly about a bleeding, dying teenager – when the history is so comprehensively diluted. I don't know what I was expecting and feel that I only have myself to blame, but I buy a couple of pricey postcards and wind through the crowds looking for the subway station.

My original idea was to walk all the way from the hotel to the best-known surviving parts of the Berlin Wall, but that still looks an awful long way off. So far I've walked over three kilometres on baking pavements on a seriously hot day. I've even stopped sweating, which I don't think can be a good thing. It's time for another train. Plus, it's lunchtime and I have a plan.

The U-Bahn whisks me the few stops east to Schlesisches Tor, just shy of the Oberbaum bridge, where a top team of international food critics – all right, TripAdvisor – suggests that I can get the best burger in all Berlin. I have to say that initial signs are not promising, as I emerge from the station on to a scrubby, traffic-choked island right underneath the railway tracks. It's the sort of location that features in drug-deal-gone-wrong stories in the local paper, and when I tell you that their own website describes Burgermeister as "a fast food joint located in a public toilet" you might be inclined to give it a miss and live another day. Still, there's a line of punters under the tracks – every day's a busy drug-deal day – and on closer inspection they are queuing outside a rather handsome vintage cast-iron kiosk that I'm prepared to believe was a toilet in a former life. I wait in line and spend five euros on an excellent cheeseburger, which I eat at a metal stand-up table overlooking the snarling traffic, while improbably whiskered and zealously tattooed kitchen hands clean up the overflowing litter bins. Re-reading my notes later, I still can't decide if all this sounds enticing or not, so for the avoidance of doubt – TripAdvisor is bang on, this is a great burger and a classic Berlin experience.

Time to move on. It's early afternoon now and it's getting ever hotter, and if I'm being strictly honest then a massive cheeseburger with a side order of diesel fumes is not the best lunch choice for a walking tour in a heatwave. But just across the bridge lies my main target of the day – the most complete surviving part of the Berlin Wall, stretching along the river between the Oberbaum bridge and Berlin Ostbahnhof station. I stroll over, glad to be closer to the water and away from the traffic, and wander along what's known as the East Side Gallery, which – with a name like that – sounds like it should be in New York. In fact, it's claimed to be the longest open-air art gallery in the world – over a kilometre from end to end – comprising murals and artworks that were painted directly onto the Wall in the years after its fall.

I'm not sure if your mental picture of the Berlin Wall, past or present, is the same as mine or if it bears any resemblance to its form and substance. It's as much symbol as edifice, with both the actual Berlin Wall and metaphorical Iron Curtain dividing East from West during a Cold War that thankfully never got too hot. For decades on the border between East and West Germany there were guard towers, barbed-wire fences, trenches, chains, minefields and no-man's land zones, but here in Berlin there was also an actual, physical wall thrown up in 1961, made of concrete and set three-and-a-half metres high. Here on the river, which formed the border, the inner wall faced East Berlin and it's this section that survived when everything else around had been torn down over the years to provide East German soldiers with a clear line of fire.

I think about that as I walk in the shadow of the Wall along an unkempt riverside promenade, with bare patches of grass and wind-scattered litter. Make it over this wall and across the river and you were in the West, but to do that you had to beat the searchlights, binoculars, bullets and patrol boats. And scale a high, smooth concrete wall before attempting any of that. Escape was tantalisingly close yet impossibly far away; the distance between East and West measured by a gunshot. It finally makes sense of a familiar lyric from a much-loved song.

In 1976 David Bowie came to West Berlin to record in the Hansa Studios, close to another section of the Wall on the west side of the city, not too far from Checkpoint Charlie. Inspired by "the most arduous city I could think of," Bowie made the album *Low*, before writing the lyrics to the song that became 'Heroes': "I, I can remember / Standing by the wall / And the guns shot above our heads / And we kissed as though nothing could fall." My friends and I would bellow out that line with Bowie – "and the guns shot above our heads" – safe in our student bars and clubs, with no walls between us and our dreams.

Many of those on the wrong side of the Wall tried and failed to escape, and kissed underneath the guard turrets as though nothing could fall. Until of course, one summer, the Wall did start to fall. Bowie had it right all along – "And the shame was on the other side / Oh, we can beat them, forever and ever / Then we could be heroes, just for one day."

The brutal symbolism of the barrier brought artists here almost the very minute that the Wall fell in the summer of 1990. The pockmarked concrete became their canvas and the open-air East Side Gallery was inaugurated that autumn by over a hundred artists from around the world, invited here to make their mark. I love this – cultural appropriation of the best kind, taking a symbol and turning it into an opposing statement. The upbeat and inventive series of works meld into each other along the wall – looping graffiti in cheery colours, kaleidoscopic swirls, cartoon figures and maze-like murals. Some of the images make me laugh out loud – the old East German Trabant car bursting through a pale blue wall or leaders Brezhnev of the Soviet Union and Honecker of East Germany locking lips in a full-on fraternal snog. Elsewhere, Miró-like figures dance to freedom and there are plenty of other poignant visual messages, subtle and not-so-subtle – snakes, dragons, skulls – alongside scrawled refrains that repeat the simplest of lines, *Wir sind ein volk* (We are one people). This could be a stale, state-sponsored memorial to the Wall and what it represented, but it's actually quite joyous – fun even.

That's it though for me. I'm done with walking for today. The long stroll beside a towering concrete wall has turned me into a human puddle. I am now thinking longingly of cold beer, which I'm led to believe Germany can help me with. I'm bound for the thing that Berlin does best of all, besides walls, which is a beer-garden. And not just any old beer-garden, but Berlin's oldest, the

43

Prater Garten in Prenzlauer Berg – making everything look better since 1837 – which by happy coincidence is only about ten minutes up the road by tram from my hotel.

I come from a pub culture in Britain, so I'm used to drinking emporiums and the place they occupy in a nation's psyche. I used to think that I couldn't live in a country where they didn't have pubs, and as they only have proper, real pubs in Britain (submit your counter-arguments in triplicate please) then Britain it was that I was destined to live out my final days in a beer-fogged stupor in the *Rat and Ferret* drinking pints of real ale with humorous names in front of a crackling fire, served by a feisty landlady of indeterminate age with hands like hams. Italian cafés, Irish bars, Spanish bodegas, Greek tavernas – all fine, obviously. I've spent many happy hours in each in Italy, Ireland, Spain and Greece, which is as it should be. But the British pub, I had assumed, was the *sine qua non* – the essential condition – of beer drinking.

Having walked under the jaunty red welcome sign and into the Prater Garten in Berlin, I see now that I am a fool. Urban beer-gardens in Britain, for the most part, are sorry adjuncts to the pub – the edge of the car park, next to the grim outside toilets, where smokers are banished and befuddled teenagers are sick into potted plants. The Prater Garten, on the other hand, is a sprawling utopia of chestnut tree-shaded benches and tables where dappled light plays through the leaves and on to the rosy cheeks of the finest specimens of Berlin's youth, drinking deceptively strong beer at inappropriate times of the day. It's a joyous sight and I join a short queue at a wooden kiosk where I scan an impenetrable beer menu – Prater Hell, Radler, Hefeweißbier – and ask for the only thing I recognise, which is a Pils. It comes in something very large that is best described as a schooner and I also order a massive pretzel, because everything is better with a pretzel the size of a child's head smeared with fiery mustard. Ideally, I need to check where the comma should go in that last sentence for absolute clarity, but I'm already on my second Pils.

The trees are keeping the sun at bay and I look around fondly at Germans enjoying themselves, thinking that perhaps I've been a bit harsh about not visiting their fine country for four decades. For the first time today I feel – what's the word? – un-hot, de-heated, dis-warmed. Shall I just have another beer, sure why not, and oh, is that the time already, six pm really, I only came in to see what it was like.

I spy sausages being served and I could stay here for dinner – heck, I could stay here for ever – but my search for the greatest Neapolitan pizza knows no borders. It's a first-night stand-by for me in a new city, if I can't be bothered – or don't have the time – to investigate the local dining scene. Where in town can I get an authentic pizza? I've eaten at the wellspring in Naples, and also in searingly good places in Bangkok, London, New York and Sydney, but the rules are always the same. The tomatoes must be San Marzano, the cheese *bufala di mozzarella*, the chewy sourdough crust flecked with charcoal because it's just out of a wood-fired oven hotter than my hotel room in Berlin in July, which is frankly impossible. A quick Google search leads me to Standard Serious Pizza, a rather slick pizzeria to which you can stagger in about fifteen minutes from the Prater Garten.

Let's be clear, in a classy joint in Berlin it's fifteen euros for some tomato- and cheese-topped dough, but Oh. My. God. That's. Good.

It would be a third of the price in Naples but because that's in Italy there would also be a complicated queuing system that makes no sense, only three choices of pizza because, well who knows, red wine served from the fridge which you're supposed to mix with Coke (again, who knows) and sweaty-armpit waiters who shout at you in an impenetrable Neapolitan dialect. It's certainly cheaper in Naples, but it can all get a bit stressful.

Here in Berlin's Standard Serious Pizza a gently spoken young man in a crisp black shirt explains in faultless English all about the provenance of the air-dried ham he's proposing to drape on my pizza, which he also tells me is made with imported artisan flour. I'm led to understand that the mozzarella cheese is from the milk of buffalo that live mollycoddled lives on the plains of Campania; there are rocket leaves flecked with dew, gathered at dawn by maidens in flowery skirts. The waiter also brings me a glass of organic wine and a green salad, and lets me muse upon the day, with only the faintest suggestion that at some point I might have to pay, leave and return to the world's hottest hotel room.

I muse and then I muse a bit more, and my musing basically takes the form of – Germany, I have wronged you, I shall be back.

Prague

But sleep? On a night like this? Franz Kafka, *The Collected Stories.*

I'D SAY THAT I'm off to Prague at the crack of dawn, only dawn cracks at around four am at this time of the year and even the hyper-efficient German railway authorities think that's too early for a train. They propose an 06.59 start if I want to get to Prague with any part of the day left to explore the city. Note that zealous erring on the side of caution – heaven forbid anyone gets that extra minute in bed so they can catch the 07.00 slackers and wastrels party train.

By the way, the hotel window-versus-air-conditioning conundrum plays itself out overnight in a typically predictable fashion. It's absolutely roasting in the room so I alternate pretty much on the hour between air-con on – relentless banging and sluicing as rocks are gaily loaded into the washing machine above my head – and window open – which is quieter but oh so much hotter. About an eleven on the dingo-sphincter scale, I'd say. There is no requirement for a sheet or covering of any kind since the hot, heavy air wraps itself like clingfilm around my torso and limbs. Even at my age, I usually prefer a covering for at least the bottom half of my body because of the possibility of the monster under the bed reaching up to touch my feet. Don't tell me you don't know what I'm talking about. But it's so ludicrously hot that

I have to settle for a sheet at around knee-level, which invites all sorts of skin-prickling alarm at the few moments I just about manage to drift off. At about five-thirty, after I've been treated to an outdoor performance by the Berlin Bin-Rolling and Waste Truck Ensemble, I call it quits for "sleeping" (as I've heard it referred to) and seek out the tea-making facilities.

There isn't a hotel experience that can't be improved by the provision of a tiny kettle, a too-small tea cup, an assortment of hot drink sachets and little plastic tear-off pots of something that once was milk before it was sterilised to the point at which it will last a thousand years. It's largely a UK thing; I'm not sure any other nation is quite as bothered as we are about the prospect of making tea in your hotel room.

A British person, checking into the no-star Hotel KidneyDisease Express, will squelch across the carpet, scattering the cockroaches, and brighten visibly the minute they spot the tea tray – "Oh look Margaret, it's really not too bad at all." If there's a cellophane-wrapped twin pack of non-branded digestive biscuits – "Biscuits Margaret! Did you tell them it was my birthday?" – the hotel can expect a glowing TripAdvisor review and a repeat annual booking.

Conversely, heaven help the five-star luxury resort where hot beverages of your choosing are delivered on request at any time of the day or night by a tray-wielding butler. Wince at the audacity of the boutique guest house where fresh milk is available in a bone-china jug and herb infusions are steeped in a fashionable glass teapot. "Well," the British person will say, down at reception at two am, pinging the little bell pointedly, "this won't do at all. Not at all I tell you." It takes a lot to get a British person to complain about something publicly – we really don't like to make a fuss – but try not putting a little kettle and some plastic milk pots in the room and see where that gets you.

Two random hot drinks sachets and a cold shower later and I'm out of the hotel and on my way down the road to the station. It's going to be another scorcher of a day if the rather worrying early morning heat is anything to go by, but it's nice and cool in the underground bowels of Berlin Hauptbahnhof. At this point, I'm also prepared to give way slightly on my views on modern train stations. Thirty years ago, breakfast would have involved avoiding the drunks at the twenty-four-hour bar and buying a bag of crisps and a can of warm Coke. Today I have a choice of early opening cafés serving *barista*-made coffee and fresh sandwiches, so the breakfast of champions it is, namely a chicken *schnitzel ciabatta* and a *macchiato*. Not German I know, but I didn't fancy an early morning pickled cucumber and a slice of cake.

The train is a rather fine air-conditioned EuroCity service with liveried seats and free newspapers, and I spend the first few minutes attempting to decipher one of the headlines with my very rusty school German. Even though I get given two of the five words for free, a story that I eventually deduce is entitled "Are you really Val Kilmer?" is still not any kind of understandable.

It takes a shade under four and a half hours to get to Prague by train from Berlin and I understand it's an attractive route, at least in the latter stages, but I confess I may have dozed off.

There's only a gentle murmur from considerate passengers, the slight hum of the air-conditioning and the soothing motion of a well-oiled train. You can hardly blame me. I wake occasionally with a start somewhere in eastern Germany as we pass yet more cement factories and, at one point, a sprawling expanse of unkempt towers, trailing cables, spouting funnels and cracked containers, where all that's missing is a klaxon and a loudspeaker shouting "Chemical plant, warning, detonation is in T-minus twenty-eight, twenty-seven …"

Beyond Dresden we hit the wide River Elbe and the views improve as the train runs along green, wooded riverbanks and past the rock-bound castles of Decin and Strekov. Then, suddenly, here we are in Prague at an entirely more reasonable time of the morning – though not, it should be said, at a more reasonable temperature, it now being thirty-four degrees and still climbing. Bleedin' hot is the technical term the meteorologists use.

I grab my backpack and follow my nose from the main station into the city centre – hoping, by the way, that I never have to ask directions *back* to the station. *Praha* (for Prague), I could have a stab at, but *hvalní nádraží* (main station) looks like nothing so much as a terrible hand at Scrabble for an English-speaking person.

It's fifteen minutes or so to my hotel for the night, where the room is not yet ready though I can leave my bags and come back later. The receptionist is not a gregarious woman; even this information is rather grudgingly imparted. She has the frosty demeanour of a woman whose toast you've eaten by mistake. She also has more pressing information to impart.

"And in the hotel, the water is broken."

I'm sorry?

"There is no water in the shower. Or the taps. There is a problem."

Riiii-ght. That *is* a problem. And when might this be fixed?

The receptionist looks at me, consults her internal protocols, remembers her training, holds both arms out, palms facing up, and says "I don't know. What can I do?"

I'm sorry? What?

"What can I do?" she repeats more loudly, as if to an imbecile.

Now I'm not a fully trained hotel receptionist with an internet connection and a working telephone system, but I can think of a few things she could try. After a bit of prompting, she ventures that "perhaps" she can call someone who might be able to help. Good plan, I agree, and leave her to it.

Now I'm here, I have to admit that I'm conflicted about Prague. I spent ages with a map of Europe when planning this trip trying to avoid stepping in the same river twice. I wanted novelty – different experiences, new adventures – while at the same time endeavouring to knock off a country a day, and it turns out that the two are mutually exclusive if A) you've been to as much of Europe as I have and B) you start in Berlin. I've been to Prague before, but all routes from Berlin lead south if you want to get through as many countries as possible in the shortest amount of time, so here I am, three years after my last visit, back in Prague.

And because I've been before, I already know that Prague is a hard city to like, especially in summer.

On the face of it, that seems like a harsh judgement for a city at the heart of Europe with a rich imperial past. Its cultural and architectural glories mostly escaped intact from the ravages of two world wars, and the capital of Czechoslovakia and, later, the Czech Republic is an agreeable city of undoubted charms and attractions. Like many such places in central Europe it might have remained in the peripheral vision of most tourists, if not for the arrival of Europe's budget airlines in the late 1990s.

As with Dublin and Barcelona before it, and Krakow and Riga after, Prague – already the purveyor of devilishly strong and cheap beer – became Stag Party capital of Europe. Not content with a night out in Coventry, stags of an adventurous persuasion started to look east for bigger thrills than tying the groom to a lamppost minus his trousers. For those of a nervous disposition – perhaps your stag night was a wine-and-cheese evening? – I do not recommend checking out pissup.com (I swear that is a genuine website), with its "Beer, babes and bullets" packages offering Hummers, Kalashnikovs, army tanks, strip-club nights and an actual "Piss-up in a brewery." I daren't even Google "hen party prague" – Hens on tour, in my limited experience, being even more outrageous than Stags – in case the images hurt my sensitive eyes. In my nearest city of York, Hens in pink sequinned nighties, with dildos strapped to their heads, roam in packs, hunting down unfortunate male buskers and middle-aged shoppers and forcing kisses and worse upon them. God only knows what they'd get up to in Prague.

Gentle reader, I realise that this is not you. It's possible you don't even know what a Hummer or a Kalashnikov is, while pissup.com's "Best-selling steak and tits activity" is probably not on your Prague itinerary. But the city centre overflows with those for whom this sounds like just the ticket. From sun-up to sun-down they clog the cobbled streets and delightful alleyways, fuelled by industrial quantities of Budvar, Pilsner Urqell and Staropramen beer, lurching from bar to bar shouting insults at the locals. Every stag-lad's whim is catered for. The answer to the question "Boys, how can we maximise our drinking opportunity in the quiet backstreets and byways of medieval Prague?" is the Beer Bike – a pedalled, wheeled drinks float for up to sixteen piss-heads that comes pre-loaded with a barrel of beer. Add electric scooter tours and guided bar crawls into the mix, apply unlimited cheap booze and scorching summer sunshine, and there you have it – total carnage (and all in the Bible by the way – "Come, let us drink heavily of strong drink; and tomorrow will be like today, only more so." Totally allowed by the Big Man.)

And let's say, dear reader, that you find yourself in Prague in summer anyway and think, well it can't be that bad. Surely he's just milking the description for comic effect? In which case let me transport you to the Old Town Square – one of Europe's most gorgeous open spaces – to which all roads in Prague eventually lead. Join the swirling crowds and observe. Do we savour the pastel-coloured Gothic buildings with their stuccoed facades and fanciful crenellations? Do we admire the thought-provoking Jan Hus memorial, honouring the religious reformer who was burned at the stake for his beliefs? Do we stroll the cobbles, picnic on artisan charcuterie underneath the shady trees and listen to the mellifluous sounds of a string quartet? No, we don't, we crowd around the giant sumo pandas, ponder a Thai massage and do our best to dodge the drunk-in-charge electric scooters and very persistent restaurant touts. We wait cheek-by-jowl in huge numbers for the hourly and underwhelming astronomical clock performance, and then join a huge queue at a faux-rustic street stall for a gristle-filled sausage and an overpriced ice cream.

As you can see, I am in something of a dilemma. Prague is lovely, but not in the Old Town in the middle of the day in summer.

If I hadn't been before, I would at least take a stroll to Prague's most famous sight, the Charles Bridge, over the Vltava river, just to say I'd seen it. It's been here since the fourteenth century and, at six hundred metres long and ten wide, it's more boulevard than bridge and the first place everyone makes a beeline for. It's lined with accomplished Baroque statues of saints that have real power – reminders that, for seventeenth- and eighteenth-century citizens of Prague, saints' lives, miracles, parables and Bible stories were part of the fabric of daily life. Even today, the commemorative plaques and statue parts show the faded gleam and wear of the touching of thousands upon thousands of hands.

There's something timeworn and reassuring about that – a relic of gentler, simpler days before Ryanair came crashing in.

But like most things in Prague in high summer, there's nothing enchanting about shuffling shoulder to shoulder over the Charles Bridge and back, squeezing past the portrait painters, buskers and jewellery sellers, and going against the flow of tour group after tour group following guides with parasols and flags. If you manage to get here early enough in the day you can still experience the bridge in a less frantic mode – the shine of ancient cobbles underfoot; the sculpted anguish of the crucifixion against a piercing blue sky; the sly yawn of a jauntily dressed boatman, waiting for a first fare; the synchronised stomp of the city street cleaners with their orange bins. But it's the middle of the day and I'm not going to sweat and stumble across the Charles Bridge. Been there, done that.

No, I'm looking for something different this time, but I need a quiet corner, away from the crowds, to grab a coffee and gather my thoughts and I know just the place. Last time I was here, I was guided by a helpful blog-post to the rooftop terrace of the Hotel U Prince, a rather spiffy boutique hotel in a venerable building right opposite the astronomical clock. It's a wonder it's not rammed, given its location, but you do rather have to trust your instincts, march in past the doorman, find the vintage elevator and follow the corridor through the restaurant on the top floor, which effort sorts the tourist wheat from the chaff. It's not that there's a dress code or anything; rather that you just need to stride in confidently and look like you know where you're going. Trust me, it's worth it. It really is a fabulous location, with views right over the milling crowds below and just the tiniest breath of a breeze ruffling the shady parasols. A sharply dressed waiter brings over a not-outrageously expensive coffee – complete with a tiny handmade chocolate, how kind – and I ponder a map of Prague and my next move.

There is apparently a Torture Museum, a Sex Machines Museum and a Beer Museum, and I don't think I'm surprised by any of these, given the sort of lads-on-tour city that Prague has become. Just for the avoidance of doubt, those are three separate museums in different parts of the Old Town, though I can't help thinking it would be far more entertaining if they were all part of the same complex and you had to start off in the Beer Museum. What could possibly go wrong in the Torture Museum and Sex Machines Museum after a few pints of Czech lager? It may also be totally unfair of me, but I can't believe that there's rigorous academic scholarship and intellectual integrity behind any of those institutions, so that's going to be a no from me.

I am vaguely tempted by the Museum of Communism, if only so that I can walk up to the entrance, knock on the door and say, "Is Len in?"

Come on, keep up.

I'm slightly more motivated by the combined Chocolate Museum and Wax Museum of Legends, where the tantalising promise, apart from chocolate, is of "lifelike wax statues of Czech celebrities" – though, without a working knowledge of Czech celebrities, how would anyone know exactly how lifelike they are?

I'll give you Ivana Trump, raise you Milos Forman and see you with Vaclav Havel, and that's me done with Czech celebrities – and to be honest I'd only have a fighting chance of recognising Ivana. I suspect they tacked on the Chocolate Museum to deal with precisely this problem for foreign tourists, and there is a lesson here for the directors of the Torture Museum, Sex Machines Museum and Beer Museum – I'm telling you, join forces guys, it works for the statues and chocolate.

Museums, I am forced to concede, are not going to do it for me today.

Ordinarily I'd just go for a walk and while away the day, with no particular destination in mind, as Prague is nothing if not beautifully set and handsomely adorned. Having painted a hellish picture of the last days of Sodom and Gomorrah, I have to confess that it's actually fairly easy to escape the worst of the Prague tourist crowds, who stick resolutely to the same few streets and squares. There are cobbled alleys and quiet courtyards, calm, onion-domed churches and locals-only neighbourhoods, all just a short walk from the centre. With a bit more effort you can find quiet parks on hillsides with open-air cafés and captivating views over town. But it's now so hot that my little artisan chocolate has become a small brown pool on the coffee spoon, which I have to drink rather than eat. I need a better plan than just tramping around aimlessly outdoors. And that's when fate intervenes.

A little red advertising arrow on the city map points me just three doors down from the hotel and up a flower-filled alley to the starting-point of the intriguing Prague Underground Tour. An hour's ramble below the streets has the twin advantages of getting away from the crowds and the sun, and for once I'm happy to follow a tour guide as a small group of us plunge into the cool depths of subterranean Prague.

While the city above-stairs reflects its fourteenth- to eighteenth-century heyday, under the tourist-tramped cobbles is another realm entirely, one that dates in part back to the first foundation of the city over a thousand years ago. It grew up around the Vltava river, in the shadow of Prague Castle, and was a key trading port long before it acquired its fancy, imperial trappings. But rivers flood, especially the Vltava – the name derived from the old German for "wild water" – and by the eighteenth century Prague had been built and rebuilt so many times that its current street level is much higher than it was centuries ago. Under the grand buildings, under the shopping streets, under the alleys, cobbles and squares, is a vast network of rooms, passages, cellars, tunnels and chambers – long-forgotten and abandoned for the most part, until rediscovered during excavations and building works.

We start in the very unlikely surroundings of a bar and club, where the staff are still cleaning up from the night before. There's a whiff of stale beer in the air and it's sticky underfoot, as we descend a circular metal staircase and emerge in a series of garishly lit cellars and tunnels that are six or seven metres underground at this point. The guide says they stretch hundreds of metres in all directions – which would take us right under the clocktower and the Old Town Square or off in the other direction towards the river and the Charles Bridge. The rough, stone-built rooms aren't simply cellars either, but are actually the remains of houses built in the 1350s and then re-purposed or lost as later generations built upwards. There are dressed stone arches and square-cut passageways leading to former service rooms and servants' quarters, as well as blocked-off entrances and staircases ending in blank walls. I touch the cool stone and try to conjure images of past inhabitants, coming and going, fetching and carrying, eating, drinking and sleeping, unaware that their descendants would literally live out their lives on top of them.

Frankly, it's all a bit creepy and doubly so in the couple of poorly lit rooms that have been turned into an art gallery – if by art gallery we mean succession of contorted figures from the Freddy Krueger School of Contemporary Sculpture. Seriously, whose idea was this? Bulbous bodies with extending claw-like hands and manic faces looming out of the shadows – great job everyone, these are exactly the sort of artworks to install in a confined underground space where the lights could go off at any minute.

Back above ground, I swing back by the hotel briefly. Mrs What Can I Do is no longer on duty and, once I get my bag in the room, I discover that the shower and the taps work just fine. Either she got over her shock at discovering that Prague has a team of dedicated water specialists on hand at a moment's notice for a hefty call-out fee – what shall we call those guys? plimbers? plambers? – or it was a mordant Czech joke at my expense. In any case, I now have a ready-made phrase for use in any blindingly obvious situation, which I look forward to using with friends and family to the point of annoyance. Jules, you're running out of petrol – Jules, the batteries have died in the TV remote – *shrugs, palms up, what can I do?*

I stroll down towards the river, thinking it might be cooler in the afternoon by the water and, by and large, this is a good plan. There's a hint of a breeze and just the sight of water always seems to make a difference. Prague has lots of bridges – not just the one you've heard of – and walking slowly down the shady riverside from the elegant Cech Bridge to the National Theatre I encounter another three of them in quick succession. I also steer largely clear of the tourist madness and still get great views – of the castle on the heights opposite, of the Neoclassical riverfront buildings, of the river cruisers, gliding swans and scudding paddle-boats, and of the crocodiles of tourists snaking across the Charles Bridge in the distance muttering "Sorry, 'scuse me, sorry, feck it's hot, sorry, 'scuse me …"

Just past the Mánes Bridge, the one before the Charles, two huge, three-metre steel cubes, each topped by a crown of spikes, stand back from the river in a small park. I wander slowly around them – one allowed to rust naturally, the other a polished stainless steel – and ponder their significance. They are unexplained, abstract, unfathomable. The best I can think of is, something to do with the Czech koruna, or crown, the national currency? I take a couple of arty photos, of metal thorns against a piercing blue sky. (Much later I find out the names of the two crowned cubes, which were designed by the architect John Hejduk – *The House of the Suicide* and *The House of the Mother of the Suicide*. They are a memorial to Jan Palach, the twenty-year-old Czech student who set fire to himself in early 1969 as a protest against the Soviet invasion of his country a year earlier. One 'house' represents Palach's mother, the other her martyred son, and the metal crown spikes are a sunburst – Palach setting himself on fire to light a resistance to oppression. Twenty years later, protests remembering his sacrifice turned into anti-Communist demonstrations that foreshadowed the student-led Velvet Revolution of 1989. I can't help thinking that I'd like to have known all this at the time, standing in front of a memorial that was clearly heartfelt by the designer but ambiguous in the extreme. Perhaps that ambiguity was the point? Again, it would have been good to know.)

In the here and now, I take a last look at the spiked cubes and finally slump down on a nearby bench under a spreading tree, listening idly to the chatter of passing strangers. The heat. The shirt-dripping, neck-burning, will-sapping heat. I have been up since long before six am. I'm exhausted. My legs are heavy and eyelids drooping as I lean back against the bench. I might as well bow to the inevitable.

No, not that. The pub.

So, you know how artisan beer halls offer nine types of IPA brewed from sun-kissed hops grown in micro-climes in the Americas and hand-picked by check-shirted yokels in straw hats? Well, in Prague, in the tree-shaded beer garden of U Fleků – a brew house in business for over five hundred years – they say "Erm, nah" and proffer a menu that says simply *pivo* (pee-vo – beer). You say "Oh go on then" and the roving waiters, laden with groaning trays, bring you the only beer they have, which is a dark malty lager with a frothy white head. It has miraculous properties, I can tell you that, whatever they put in it. The waiters keep bringing the trays round, and I keep saying "Go on then" and, some time later, perhaps the same day, it's hard to tell, I get a bill that looks like it was for one tiny glass of IPA in a London hipster bar.

Look, if you don't want me to keep ending my days in a beer garden, you have to stop making it so atrociously hot.

U Fleků is well on its way to the top spot, nudging out yesterday's number one, Berlin's Prater Garten. For a start, this tree-covered courtyard of an historic inn is entirely shaded – there's not so much as a shaft of sunlight. I'm cool, possibly for the first time in my life, or so it seems. More to the point, waiters are actually bringing me beer, rather than me having to go and fetch it, and when they do they simply make a little chalk mark on my wooden table so they know how many to charge me for when I leave. An unscrupulous person – a bad travel writer, say – might erase one of those marks, entirely by accident. Anyway, as I say, well on its way to the coveted number one spot, when a man in coordinating yellow-and-brown-check waistcoat and trousers turns up, clutching an accordion.

I shy at this intrusion, in the manner of a skittish mustang startled by the arrival of a rattlesnake. This smacks of the

Peruvian pan-pipe band or the restaurant *mariachi* trio – inevitable but undesirable when all you really want to do is eat and drink in peace. Enforced musical accompaniment is not really my thing. I have no truck with the pub diddly-dee group, for example, ever since the one in Scotland where the singer prefaced every new song with the line "And here's another one about murdering the English." That was an awkward night. I'm also the man who once refused to pick up a hitch-hiking backpacker – and I *always* pick up hitch-hiking backpackers – because he was flagrantly carrying a pair of bongos. Not in my car matey.

Captain Accordion starts off at the far end of the beer-garden and all seems typical – the wheezy tunes, the muted applause, the proffered cap. But the dark frothy lager is clearly doing its stuff because, as he moves around the tables, I realise I am consulting deeply buried feelings of an unknown nature. Is that, could that be – enjoyment? The Captain is playing an instrument that is traditional in these parts, and instead of being irritating – pan-pipes in Leicester Square, for example – it seems entirely appropriate. A rich cascade of harmonies tumbles from the accordion; melodies from another era, another world. The lilting notes of polkas, airs and jigs dance among the leaves and bounce off the growing number of empty beer glasses. The Captain rolls and smiles his way around the tables and people seem genuinely pleased to hear him play – and so play he does, as the waiters chalk their marks and I slip into a beer-calmed state of grace.

Tomorrow, Vienna. Tonight, a tune-filled farewell to a city I really need to give another chance. Just not in summer in a heatwave.

Vienna

This means nothing to me, Oh, Vienna. Ultravox.

I AM DECIDEDLY chirpy, no question about it, largely on account of the soothing properties of Czech beer and the subsequent embrace of Keats' soft embalmer of the still midnight. Got a bit *pivo*-ed, had a great kip, is basically what I'm saying.

Also, today's train is an absolute joy. For a start, the 09.20 Regiojet service from Prague to Vienna has a much more civilised departure time and a very cheery uniformed attendant to welcome me aboard. Awaiting me is a reserved window seat facing in the direction of travel. There is a free bottle of water and a complimentary Czech newspaper, though having been burned by the whole Val Kilmer business I decline that. Next up, a few minutes into the journey, is a proffered cup of tea, which, on inspection, is mint tea made with actual mint leaves, and honey – honey I tell you! – is optional. As I've paid nineteen euros for the ticket for the entire four-hour journey, this strikes me as remarkably generous and I await whatever comes next. A massage and a hotdog surely? A footbath with some of those nibbly little fish? Not quite, but there is more tea or fresh coffee on demand, a flower display in the spotlessly clean train toilets, while sushi, ordered from Cheery Guard, costs a ridiculous two euros, and the same again for a chia-and-mango smoothie. Every seat has a power socket, the wifi works, and the service is prompt and friendly.

As a British person, I find all this both puzzling and irresistibly attractive. Good-value tickets? Sushi and smoothies? Tea and honey? On a train! I don't really do national pride, so while on the one hand acknowledging that we literally invented trains, I think it's fair to say that British train travel is uniformly awful. In the UK, we no longer value our railways or the people who work on them and ride on them. We're herded onto ancient rolling stock, and treated entirely as 'customers' to be gouged financially and not passengers to be transported safely and comfortably. Services are delayed and cancelled with such ironic regularity that they could be printed up in timetables. We might have known it would never go well after the initial trip on George Stephenson's pioneering Liverpool and Manchester Railway in 1830. All on the same day, the world's first locomotive-hauled passenger railway service also saw the world's first train-on-train collision and the world's first railway fatality, as the unfortunate local MP, William Huskisson, contrived to get himself run over by Stephenson's famous engine, the Rocket.

But clearly, modern train travel can be done properly, in the Czech Republic at least. Let's hope this service hasn't somehow slipped through the net, avoiding the attention of Europe's Fat Controller, until one day the alarm goes off in his office, the big red button starts flashing and Regiojet receive a stern warning that This Sort Of Thing can't be allowed to continue. But until then, I thoroughly recommend the highly comfortable and relaxing sushi- and smoothie-fuelled ride from Prague to Vienna.

We clatter at high speeds through rolling Czech wheat fields and along somnolent rivers, stopping at occasional stations for towns with insufficient vowels in them. At Brno, the largest town on the route, there's a view of the impressive twin-towered cathedral from the train; with more time, on another day, I'd jump off and have a look around. Another half an hour, past the Czech town of Breclav, we've crossed the border into Austria, where the guard pops along to see if I need any more tea and, almost apologetically, asks if I would be so kind – if it's all right with me and he entirely understands if not – to show him my ticket. I do so, and it occurs to me that this is the first time this has happened so far.

I've travelled from Berlin to Prague and now almost to Vienna – three days, three countries, two international borders – and until now no one has checked my ticket, let alone asked to see a passport. This is quite a thing, to be a European citizen (which is really how I think of myself) in the European Union, with full freedom of movement across twenty-seven member states. You get used to the lack of borders, guards, ticket checks and passport stamps; you settle back in your train seat and don't even notice that no one is asking you to prove your status and justify your journey. I realise that the two things are different – that no one's been asked for a ticket or passport, whatever their nationality. And I accept that e-tickets and online seat reservations have removed some of the on-board paperwork.

Even so – you would think you would have to produce a passport and a ticket more frequently than this. But, as a modern European, it hasn't really occurred to me until this point. I'm used to getting on trains in one country and getting off in another without formalities. I'm used to the absence of hard borders. I'm used to frictionless travel. Those all seem like good things to be used to.

But I can't help thinking that this will all change now the UK has committed its colossal act of national self-harm – sorry, "Taken back control and left the overbearing tyranny of the EU." We've left the club for the single dubious benefit of being able to have a British blue passport and not a burgundy-coloured EU one. In future, I'll be sitting in a train seat feeling small and British – not large and European – and wondering if I have to fish my travel documents out of my bag at every approach of a conductor. The thought of it makes me rather cross.

To avoid tramping around Vienna looking for accommodation, which would at this point make me even more combustible, I have booked a hotel in advance not too far from the station. But not too far from the station is still far enough when it comes to toting a backpack through sizzling city streets. Every news website and weather app is now gaily informing me that we are in a record-breaking heatwave, with temperatures climbing to disagreeable heights in every city on my route. Weather warning symbols have changed from the little yellow and red triangles to a devil-with-pitchfork icon, while maps of central Europe have lost all national borders and are just coloured in a fiery red, overlaid with the single word "Scorchio."

I realise that, as an English person, I have little authority in these matters. While we can talk all day about the weather with the best of them, we really don't have any weather to talk about. We're a northern, maritime island nation, warmed by the Gulf Stream and sheltered by the Continent – English weather is a bit fresh, it gets a little windy now and again, it's cloudy and overcast a lot of the time, and it rains a lot. Winters are mild and snow increasingly uncommon – there have only been ten years since 1960 when snow has laid on the ground in the south of England on Christmas Day. Extreme weather events are so rare that we still talk about a hurricane that happened in 1987.

The summers are no better. Do you know what the official definition of a heatwave is in the UK, as determined by the Met Office? Three days of temperatures over twenty-five degrees Celsius – three days! twenty-five! – which to put it into perspective is the sort of weather in which a Spaniard will consider taking off their winter coat. A nice summer's day for English people is when the temperature reaches a heady eighteen degrees, you can undo the top button of your shirt and maybe think about an ice cream. At twenty-five degrees in England, the entire country goes mad and grinds to a halt as businessmen chug beer and strip down to their boxers in Hyde Park and my mother turns off her central heating and opens the lounge window a crack.

You might be forgiven then for thinking that I'm protesting a tad too much about the weather – what does an English person know about heatwaves? – but I'm telling you, Vienna is aflame and this is not ideal backpack-carrying weather.

If I was my Dad, I'd be grand. A veteran of six continents, he travelled everywhere with a khaki safari suit, slacks and a suitcase and somehow managed to look effortlessly cool whatever the provocation. A sort of George Clooney of the technical education world. He actually had one of those little battery-operated, hand-held fans, which he kept in his zipped, tartan, compartmentalised overnight bag. I myself on the other hand am more in the mould of a *School of Rock*-era Jack Black, with a dishevelled wardrobe and luggage that is described on the catwalk as "Shabby Urban." Today I am modelling a light, flappy, buttoned, untucked cotton shirt which disobligingly rides up my back with every stride. After five minutes or so I'm essentially carrying the pack against my bare back, with the shirt sides gathered somewhere under my armpits. You don't even want to know what's going on in my armpits. The ageing backpack squelches where it touches, as perspiration adds an entirely unwelcome layer of lubricant. You could grease a team of sumo wrestlers with what's pouring off my body. There are deep sweat marks under the shoulder straps, another wet band at my waist, and the top of the pack chafes against my increasingly sunburned neck. It's like having a large, sweaty toddler clasped to your back, demanding that horsey has another gallop, when all that horsey wants to do is ditch its rider and drink deeply from Daddy's Magic Medicine in the fridge.

It's as unpleasant as it sounds, but I am neither downbeat nor dejected because the hotel I have booked is called the AllYouNeedHotelVienna, and here it is looming into sight, after a fifteen-minute slog from the station. It only costs forty-nine euros* a night but, given its name, is almost certainly going to be providing me with ice baths on the hour, a swimming pool, an assistant to follow me around with a fan, and a limitless supply of iced tea. (*Examines the small print and facilities on arrival and is astonished – astonished! – to find that the AllYouNeedHotelVienna has been falsely advertised and would, in fact and probably in law, be better named the WhatDoYouExpectForFortyNineEurosANightHotel.) I should have that known something was up from the elision of the words in the name – saving money on the printing I expect.

It turns out that this is student accommodation for much of the year, with the rooms made available for tourists in the summer. Students are not what you'd call the finest custodians of other people's property, so this doesn't bode well. There's clunky kit furniture, a creaky metal-framed bed, and chips and dents in the wall-plaster that indicate a good time has been had in here at some point – possibly involving golf clubs and catapults. But no matter, I'm not hanging around, as I have a city to see and a shade under twenty hours to do so.

This could be a daunting task in the wrong hands. Vienna is not just a city but a former imperial capital, inhabited since at least 500 BC, and top-dog residence for the Habsburgs, the Holy Roman Empire, the Austrian and then the Austro-Hungarian

71

Empire. A noted centre of art, philosophy and music, it has palaces, museums and galleries coming out of its regal and refined ears, as well as a soaring Gothic cathedral, the clip-cloppy Spanish Riding School and a famous opera house the size of a small nation. There's the handsome location on the River Danube and an inordinate number of parks and gardens. There's also the considerable legacy of Schubert, Strausses I and II, Mozart, Beethoven, Freud, Trotsky, Wittgenstein, Fritz Lang, Graham Greene and *The Third Man*. Midge Ure and Ultravox too, come to think of it. In short, there's more to see here than you could possibly get around in a year, let alone a day, but fortunately for Vienna, the city is in the very capable – but entirely shallow – hands of yours truly.

I have to let you into a terrible secret. On the whole – and with a few honourable exceptions – jobbing travel writers and bloggers don't know very much in advance about the places that they visit. You gain some familiarity over the years, if you keep going back to the same destinations, but most newspaper features, magazine articles and blog-posts are written by writers whose only qualification is that they've been sent there by their boss or simply liked the idea of going. I'd never set foot in Scandinavia, Sicily, Washington DC or Hong Kong before I was asked to write books about them, which sounds crazy when you set it down like that, but it is – or at least used to be – a perfectly normal state of affairs. I've been on foreign travel press trips with newspaper motoring correspondents whose turn it was for the freebie, and read in-depth blogs on countries by gap-year travellers who turn out to have spent two weeks there. This isn't necessarily to denigrate those practices. If writers are good at their job, they'll do plenty of research, talk to the right people and go to the right places and, when you eventually read what they've written, you'll feel like you're in the hands of someone who knows what they're talking about. Travel writers should earn your trust by travelling in the right way and writing well – and my personal view is that it's always as much about the writing as it is the travelling. In fact, I'd go as far to say that the travel isn't the important part in travel writing. Anyone can get on a train to Vienna. But not everyone can write, and you do need to be able to do that well to be a travel writer. Travellers who write, it was once said, worked for Lonely Planet. Writers who travel got the Rough Guides gig and, happily for me all those years, they thought I could write.

Enjoy a fleeting acquaintance with cities and countries is one of things I do best then. I never have the time to stay for a week, a month or a year, getting to know the "real" destination, wherever that may conceal itself. Wherever I go, I usually have a job to do and a couple of days to do it – checking out restaurants, hitting the main museums, sampling the street life, searching for an angle for a story or a hook for a feature article. We can debate whether that's right or wrong – Why should you trust writers who don't really know the places they visit? Discuss – but it is mostly the case that I show up to a place that I don't know very well (if at all), shoot around and ship out. That's my working practice; I pretty much always run on borrowed time in any place I visit. It's no different today.

What I know about Vienna is contained in the hundred and fifty words or so I rattled off earlier, covering the historical and cultural highlights that any reasonably interested person could uncover in ten minutes on the internet. I've been here twice before, decades apart, once on my teenage InterRail trip (no memories) and much later on a press trip to go the opera (terrible memories, involving turning up woefully under-dressed and having to wear a multi-coloured kipper tie and jacket with giant lapels provided by the outraged management). Basically, I know nothing about Vienna while knowing enough to know that there's no point in trying to see the city in under a day. My own rules preclude it in any case.

Instead, I'm going to dismiss a thousand years of culture in one of Europe's most important cities – shallow, I warned you – and go and have a look at a couple of off-piste things that popped up during a quick Google search on the train here. Trust me, I'm a travel writer, it'll be fun.

First up is a quick Metro ride to Wien Mitte station and then a ten-minute walk from the grand, monumental buildings of the city centre into a quiet residential neighbourhood, bounded by the curve of the River Danube. I am curious to see the river in any case, just to satisfy my curiosity, and stroll along between a couple of bridges while I get my bearings.

Disappointingly, and despite what you may have heard, the Danube is not blue. Johann Strauss (II, son, not father) has a lot to answer for here, but he wrote his famous waltz ("On the beautiful blue Danube") in 1866 to cheer up the locals after Austria had been defeated in war by Prussia. I think we have to concede that calling it "On the miserable muddy Danube" would not have lifted spirits in the same way. Even so, walking along a muddy river on a hot day is still an excellent thing to do – zest for life, breeze in your hair and all that – and as the sun is currently glinting and the water sparkling, even the sluggish, drab Danube appears to be raising its game.

I am looking for a building known as the Hundertwasserhaus on a street called Kegelgasse, just a little way back from the river. I'd say it's a hidden gem, if it wasn't for the fact that that's a terrible travel cliché. If I'd abseiled down a five-hundred-metre-high cliff, crossed a fraying rope bridge and swum the barracuda-infested Danube then I might just be allowed to use it. As we can see though, I came on the metro, which also doesn't make the Hundertwasserhaus "off the beaten track." Travel bloggers love that one too, usually to describe a destination so little known and fiendishly difficult to reach that it's in every guidebook and travel article ever written. You'll know it when you get there because it will be packed with people getting off tour buses and out of rental cars, clutching guidebooks and travel articles.

However, when I say you can't miss the Hundertwasserhaus you can take me at my travel-writing word. It doesn't so much stand on the street as pour along it, in a sinuous wave of colour that shakes a fist at conservative Vienna and shouts, "Baroque? Neoclassical? No chance, this is what the people want!".

Like Antoni Gaudí in Barcelona before him, the naturalistic Austrian artist born Friedrich Stowasser but known popularly as Hundertwasser abhorred a straight line and standard geometry of any kind. Here he is on the subject, firm but fair – "The straight line leads to the downfall of our civilisation." Couldn't be clearer, no fan of the horizontal or perpendicular. He was an individualistic, anti-authoritarian environmentalist, whose art and architecture spoke volumes about his belief that man and nature should be equal partners. (Yes, I looked all this up later – I do occasionally do some work you know.)

Hundertwasser thought that buildings should be built for humans; that trees should be planted wherever they can, including in rooms and on roofs; and that windows have a duty to be painted and embellished. "Some people say that houses consist of walls," said Hundertwasser; "I say houses consist of windows," which is fine if you're an artist but a trickier motto to live by if the city of your birth invites you to design an apartment building. I'd like to have been in the planning meeting when that went through.

"So Hundy – can we call you Hundy? – talk us through these plans again. Windows, we're all good, plenty of those. No two the same size or shape obviously, but hey! you're the artist. But where are the walls and the doors, for example?"

"Uneven" doesn't even begin to describe the building I'm looking at, which was finished in the 1980s. It's what Hundertwasser himself called a "divine melody," in harmony with nature – and about as far removed from the rest of Vienna as is possible. What you get in practice is an undulating façade of teetering levels, ceramic swirls and vibrant tiles. The storeys are picked out in pastel colours, with apartments divided by wavy boundary lines and pockmarked with too many windows – like a child has been allowed to draw them on. Trees and shrubbery sprout from the roofline and balconies, while at ground level a maw-like cave supported by ceramic columns draws you in and under the building.

Traditional architects, of course, hate it, but what do they know? I love it – there's the same sense of fun you get with the *modernista* buildings in Barcelona, even though neither Hundertwasser nor Gaudí were exactly a barrel of laughs themselves. Gaudí went mad, lived in his studio, wandered unkempt around Barcelona muttering to himself and was killed when he got knocked down by a tram. Hundertwasser's idea of a big night out was a small glass of sherry while shouting at a straight line. You wouldn't have wanted to have been stuck with either of them at a dinner party, that's all I'm saying. This building though is hilarious and I walk around smiling and stroking the surfaces I can touch, wondering what it would be like to live in such a joy-encrusted apartment. You'd be hacked off by the tourists outside in the first ten minutes I expect, but then you do get to cook, eat, wash and sleep in something that looks like it was designed by Spongebob Squarepants.

I've got one more offbeat attraction to visit and, as this one turned out well, I'd say my day in Vienna is looking all right so far. First, though, I want a sit-down and a cup of coffee and I have a plan for that too, which involves heading for the Café Sacher, where I am reliably informed – no, not just by TripAdvisor, but by Cake People – that they serve the best chocolate cake in the world. Come on, a recommendation like that, you would, wouldn't you? It's across town so I wend my way back to the Metro, jump off at Karlsplatz and wander up past the State Opera House, scene of my humiliation many years ago. Even now, the sight of a swan or a lake brings me out in hives. While I'm here, I revise my description of it – it's not the size of a small country, it's actually the size of a medium-sized nation and takes ages to walk around, though partly because I get side-tracked by the pavement plaques honouring the composers that Vienna is known for. I check out the plaque for Strauss. Yep, he's still claiming the Danube is blue.

At the Café Sacher – part of a glam hotel of the same name – there's a queue, but it moves fairly swiftly, tumbling me through a gleaming, brass-handled door and straight into the 19th century. A waiter in a red velvet waistcoat and black bow tie shows me to a small marble table in a crimson-walled salon, hung with dripping chandeliers and stacked with gilt-framed oil paintings and old photographs. It's the sort of place where I start rifling my wallet, checking I've still got credit cards in case the several hundred euros in cash isn't enough. We are talking old-school Vienna, from the courteous service to the silver tableware, but the Café Sacher is part of a more relaxed Viennese tradition too – the daily visit to the *kaffeehaus*. It might look – all right, is – fancy, but having a sit-down, a slice of cake and a cup of coffee in a grand place like this is considered part and parcel of the local working day rather than a decadent luxury. There's even a word for it – *gemütlich* – which basically means relaxed and easy-going, with time for the finer things in life.

So now I'm down with the fact that chocolate-cake eating is essentially a public good – a duty if you will – I apply myself to the menu.

To be honest, there's no point. There's only one thing to have, the clue is in the name. *Sachertorte*, the rich, dense chocolate cake that they have been serving here since 1832. It comes in a deceptively dainty wedge, accompanied by a disconcertingly squirty Mr Whippy-style cream and topped with a monogrammed disc of chocolate. I nibble and taste and spoon away – spoon on its own? spoon and fork? I never know – and the *sachertorte* disappears inside me as cherubim and seraphim sing and frolic and world peace is declared. Best chocolate cake in the world? Mmmm, caaaake, is what I say.

There's a whole ritual to this too. The cake has been delivered on a silver tray with a long-handled copper jug of Turkish-style coffee and some tiny dusted cubes of Turkish delight. Just in case I haven't yet had my entire month's allowance of sugar. Boy, that's good coffee, the muddy sort you have to strain through your teeth, mainlining the caffeine. I order another pot, flick through the history of the café in a faux-vintage newspaper and eventually – *gemütlich*ed to the brim – call for the bill. At this point, saying "It's not cheap" seems pointless – it's Vienna for goodness sake – but there certainly seems to have been a misplacing of the decimal point. I never intended to buy shares in the café, just come in for a drink, but there you go. For good measure they have you exit by the gift shop, where you can take out mortgages to buy *sachertorte* to go, gift-wrapped and vajazzled like Christmas parcels from Harrods.

With gilt-lined cake sloshing around inside me, I waddle the short distance to the monumental gate of the Burggarten, once the Emperor Franz Josef's private garden, first laid out in 1818 but opened to the public a century later. Emperors and palaces, not really my thing, I have to admit. The vast acres of formal rooms stuffed with horsehair armchairs and inlaid cabinets; the bewigged portraits, the golden dinner services, the stench of privilege – I'm squarely with the iconoclastic first edition of the *Rough Guide to France*, which I remember fondly started one of its chapters with the phrase "The Palace of Versailles is foul from every aspect."

But I do like a good garden, and especially once it's been thrown open to the plebs – an entirely honourable social status by the way, from the Latin *plebeian*, a free Roman citizen. Don't ever be offended by being called a pleb – it's a badge of honour. Once, you could only peer through the gate and over the wall at the royal Burggarten, but now they let in any old riff-raff, so I saunter through the gate. The garden itself – more an urban park – is not really the reason I'm here though. I read an article on the train that suggested a day in Vienna wasn't complete without a butterfly landing on your hand, which seems like a philosophy to get behind. And the Palmenhaus at the Burggarten is a soaring glasshouse full of butterflies, where for the princely sum of seven euros you can lurk as long as you want and indulge your new passion for butterfly-handling.

Every word for butterfly is delightful – *papillon* in French, *farfalla* in Italian, *mariposa* in Spanish, *borboleta* in Portuguese – but now I've discovered it I'm giving my vote to the German, *schmetterling*, a gorgeous, dancing word that seems just right for the ethereal creatures that flit between the palms and exotic blooms. It comes from an old German word *schmetten* (cream) and the same folk belief that gives us the English word; ie, that butterflies eat butter, milk and cream. German gets a bad rep for its lengthy compound words, but start looking up translations for insects and animals and there are some real beauties – from *fledermaus* (flutter mouse, bat) to *nacktschnecke* (naked snail, slug).

The *schmetterlings* live in, naturally, the Schmetterlinghaus, where it's breath-sappingly humid. I follow a circular, one-way path that winds through jungle fronds, creepers and sculpted rocks, and I strain to see the butterflies at first, because the plants themselves are remarkable. Half of them look like they could eat you, and most are incredibly rich in colour, with a mix of razor-sharp leaves, spiked stems, protruding stamens and filaments, and groaning seed pods. Stand still long enough though and here come the *schmetterlings*, landing here and there, tumbling away at the slightest movement, disguising themselves cannily and then opening up to reveal wings of the deepest blue, red and orange. As my eyes grow accustomed, I pick out movement and then stillness, peering down onto the gravel to find camouflaged butterflies, which then wheel up, flitter and fall to a new resting-place – including, to everyone's delight, on arms, heads and T-shirts. Make a move and off they fly again, while others stay aloof, circling overhead and hiding amongst the plants. Each butterfly is extraordinarily delicate, which of course makes them vulnerable – it's always a shock to realise that most butterflies only live a couple of weeks, though larger tropical species like these might last several months, sheltered as they are from the weather and predators.

An hour goes by quite easily, here among the *schmetterlings*. This really is a perfect place, and while I know I could have tramped around a couple of imperial museums and seen some Lipizzaner horses today, I think a wonky artist's house and a butterfly garden have been two great choices. I feel I've experienced a bit more of Vienna that I might have done – plus, there was the cake, let's not forget the world's best cake.

Back in the hotel, after a shower, a round of golf and some catapult practice, I ask at the front desk for a local dinner recommendation.

"What do you like to eat? Austrian food?"

Now I know the answer to this. It's no.

I once had an Austrian student stay at my house and to say thank you she promised to cook a speciality from her home nation, whose name and ingredients she refused to divulge. It seemed churlish to refuse so we let her at it. After about three hours she emerged from the kitchen – which, by the way, looked as if there had been an explosion in a flour and egg factory – with a frying pan that looked as if someone had thrown up in it. This apparently was *käsespätzle* – a sort of Austrian mac-and-cheese – that managed to be both rubbery and glutinous at the same time, without any discernible taste or flavouring. I gather that if you're a particularly racy, avant-garde Austrian cook you could add a dash of paprika, which is the only spice they seem to allow, but she had gone for the full-on, taste-free traditional version. Like most traditional Austrian dishes it was beige and cream in colour – basically, my mum's lounge on a plate. She piled it high and wouldn't take no for an answer when it came to second helpings.

Before I can come up with a diplomatic reply, the receptionist adds, "There's the Naschmarkt, it's only a few minutes down the road, you can get all different types of food there. Thai, Chinese, Lebanese."

Well hello Naschmarkt.

It started out as a dairy market in the 1780s – it says here – but has since morphed into the biggest general market in town, with a full mile of stalls between Karlsplatz and Kettenbruckengasse. You go there to buy tie-dye wraps, knock-off soccer shirts, cheap shoes, beads and jewellery, slogan T-shirts and big pants. On Saturdays, there's a flea market where antique dealers mix it with people who have emptied the contents of granny's attic in the vain hope that someone wants to buy a stuffed antelope head or a chandelier. I've missed all this but I haven't missed the food, which it turns out is the best reason to go to the Naschmarkt.

There's fruit and veg, some butchers and bakers, and a couple of high-end delis, but they are outgunned by the huge array of street food stalls and snack joints selling Asian, Italian, North African and Middle Eastern snacks and produce. I see falafels and samosas, pizza slices and kebabs, marinaded olives and stuffed flatbreads, and when I see those things I generally know that everything is going to turn out just fine. There are restaurants and bars, too, that look elsewhere for inspiration – open all day, but also buzzing at night, when the fairy lights come on and the open window seats and outdoor tables are filled with drinkers and diners. It's more Asian night market than central European street market, with some brilliant places to eat and then glasses of *Prosecco* and DJ sets in the bar along the alley. Even just writing that doesn't make it sound like you're in Vienna at all, or at least in the traditional Vienna found in tourist brochures and guidebooks.

After a recce – up and down the market aisles twice to make sure I haven't missed anywhere – I settle on Li's Cooking, a likely looking Vietnamese joint where red-faced diners are tucking into dangerously spicy bowls of *pho* soup. I do like a bowl of *pho*, but then I do like to retain the inner lining of my cheeks and the skin on my tongue. I settle instead for Vietnamese tofu-stuffed summer rolls, a plate of Malaysian pepper beef with fried rice and a large glass of wine, all for twenty euros, which for Vienna is pretty darned good. Yes, about the price of a slice of cake, since you ask.

Meandering back to the hotel, I find a quiet side street lined with yet more outdoor cafés and settle into one, musing on the fact that Vienna really is not the stuffy, starchy city of lazy reputation. You know how it goes. The Germans run a shit-hot train system, the Czechs make great beer, the Austrians are uptight and have terrible food. The British make snap cultural judgements and then invade and exploit you, that sort of thing. Of course, I know that none of these observations are remotely representative (well, maybe the British one is), but it's easy to cling to familiar national stereotypes as a sort of comfort blanket every time we travel. We know exactly what this place is going to be like – we know what to expect from Austria because we've read the newspapers and seen the TV shows and haven't ever stopped to think if that's the whole story. We don't even know there is another story to be told beyond the familiar stereotype.

I do it myself, half the time without realising that I've already made my mind up about a place. For instance, the café waiter brings me – on his recommendation – a glass of Austrian red wine and I find myself thinking, who knew there was such a thing? But why wouldn't there be Austrian red wine? Vienna is on the same latitude as central France. They even make wine in England for God's sake (I appreciate that all French readers are now clutching their pearls and recoiling in horror at the very thought). What's so astounding about a decent glass of Austrian red, served a short walk from a night market where they serve an entirely authentic spicy noodle soup?

I'm with the late, lamented chef, traveller and writer Anthony Bourdain – "The more I travel, the less I know about anywhere," he said, and I still don't know very much about Vienna, it seems, beyond the clichés.

Enough self-flagellation. Lesson learned. Bed – and Bratislava – beckons.

Bratislava

Cabbage is best after it is reheated seven times. Slovak proverb.

HERE'S HOW MY thought process goes this morning. Higher is cooler, we all know that. Baking hot on the plains and in the river valleys, a distinct chill in the air on the top of a mountain. Ask anyone who's ever climbed Everest, they'll tell you. For this reason, I fondly imagine that climbing to the heights of Bratislava Castle – eighty-five metres above town – will reward me with a refreshing breeze that will play around my limbs like gaspy little breaths from a cavorting angel.

Reader, it does not.

By the time I get to the top of the steps, I drip from every orifice I know about and quite a few that are new to me. If there are angels, I am sorry to report that they are not cavorting, they are slumped in an ungainly heap of wings and halos, unable to emit so much as a celestial squeak. Saint Peter must be doing his nut – "Guys, come on, get up! There's flying and gasping to be done, this fella looks like he's going to cark it at any minute."

Meanwhile, it turns out that breathing is also no longer something I can continue to take for granted. My lungs have decided that it's more in the way of a luxury and that oxygen is now to be carefully rationed; I can have a bit more later for a treat. I consult Calves, Thighs and Chest, but they are basically in the process of shutting down, clearing out their desks and switching off the lights. Checking the weather app on my phone, I see it's now thirty-eight degrees – just over a hundred Fahrenheit – which I am forced to concede is not really tramping-up-a-steep-hill weather.

Mind you, this leg of the trip nearly never happened because of the mysterious and unhelpful cancellation of my planned train from Vienna to Bratislava this morning, "because construction". Construction of the train, the track, the station or the entire city of Bratislava, there is no way of knowing, because each rephrased query at the ticket counter about the cancellation simply elicits another bemusing variant of "because construction." There is no help to be had at the counter about alternative trains. I am instead treated to an involved explanation, mostly in German so I may have got some of this wrong, about how they are in the business of selling train tickets and not providing train information. There is apparently another counter where their training has been in the matter of providing information and not selling tickets and that, in this counter clerk's opinion, is where I should take up the question of the cancelled train to Bratislava.

I really do want to go to Bratislava – the whole one-day, one-country theme of the trip depends on it. But I really don't want to go and stand in another queue and have another impenetrable conversation with a distinctly unhelpful rail employee. Luckily, I am a guidebook writer by profession and if there's one thing guidebook writers know how to do it is to study a public transport timetable written in an unfamiliar language and make head and tail of it. I couldn't count the hours – days, weeks – that I have stood in foreign train and bus stations and copied down timetables. Pre-internet, it was the only way to get hold of the information; even now, I'd still rather trust the timetable posted at the station than the app on my phone. If you've ever scanned those practical bits of a guidebook – travel details, getting there and away, need to know – and wondered how they are sure that there are seventeen daily departures from A to B via C that take an hour (two hours on Sun in Aug), five will get you ten that some poor sap has counted them off a timetable while trying to decipher if the asterisk means "Only on Tuesday if there's an R in the month, except school days."

Here's where the *European Rail Timetable* would have come in handy, so that's definitely a note to self. Instead, I shimmy on over to the big printed timetable displays in Vienna Hauptbahnhof and set to work. It's a shame you missed it, it must have been a delight to see, a professional at work, running his finger down the serried lines of station names and departure times, wringing sense and clarity from the overwhelming number of trains that pass through Vienna each day. And trying to remember the days of the week in German and ferreting out that "hl. st." apparently means "main station" in Slovakian.

It seems that there is an alternative train in an hour or so which goes not to Bratislava hl. st. but to Bratislava-Petržalka. Day saved, trip back on. A quick jump for joy and time for a swift cup of coffee in Vienna's very grand station you might think? Well I've been caught like this before, as has anyone who has ever bought a plane ticket to Barcelona (Girona), got off the aircraft expecting to see the Sagrada Família and discovered that they are at least a hundred kilometres from Barcelona and in the queue for the transfer bus that takes another two hours. Never trust the hyphen or the parenthesis is my advice when it comes to destinations.

At the train information counter, (not quite) all is revealed. They are confident about the location of Bratislava-Petržalka, which is "Two kilometres from city centre." Not a different region then, but still further than you'd want to walk with a backpack in a heatwave. Am I reassured by the extra piece of information that "There is bus to centre – probably"? I am not.

Maybe it's lost in the translation, and perhaps the "probably" is less woolly and more encouraging in the original German. Then again, you should never overestimate the European regard for the niceties of customer service. In Britain, if a shop says it opens at nine am, then it's entirely fair to queue up outside beforehand and start getting twitchy at one minute to nine if you can't see any signs of movement inside. In Italy, on the other hand, I once saw a sign in a shop window that said "Open eleven am – perhaps" (*forse*). In Spain, bus schedules are more in the way of a suggestion than a promise; you certainly wouldn't make firm plans on the basis of a departure timed for nine am. I'd add twenty percent and think yourself lucky if you get away for nine-forty. And in Portugal I went into a restaurant at lunchtime where – despite the sign saying "Aberto, Bem-vindo" (Open, Welcome) – the owner had his head in his arms on the counter.

When he heard the door open, he looked up, rolled his eyes and tutted at the intrusion, pointed lethargically to a table, sighed and switched the lights on. Tricky business, customer service – you can't rely on things working as they do at home.

Possibly because I am a seasoned traveller, or more likely because what's the choice?, I buy a ticket and jump on the later train for the hour's ride from Vienna to Bratislava-Petržalka. I figure that I'll worry about that "probably" when I get there.

It's only a short trip but surprisingly scenic as the train runs for much of the way along the River Danube across a strikingly green and forested landscape. There are wooden buildings and shacks at intermittent points, which look like fishermen's huts and boat-houses, and then we're soon rattling through faceless housing and tower-blocks on the outskirts of Bratislava. Petržalka, I presume – which I later discover is sometimes known as the "Bratislava Bronx." Again, they don't mention that before they sell you a ticket there.

As I'm sure you will all be using this book to plan your own madcap European rail adventure at some point, here's a useful travel tip.

If you ever find yourself at Bratislava-Petržalka "because construction," there is indeed a bus to the centre, the number eighty, which has a stop right outside the station. You simply jump on the bus and then jump off again when the angry bus driver shouts and points at the ticket machine by the bus shelter, which has a huge variety of entirely incomprehensible tickets available. You buy a random ticket because all the instructions are in Slovakian and then turn round to watch Angry Driver drive off, laughing maniacally. Then get on the next number eighty, whose driver will show no interest in your hard-won ticket, and get off ten minutes later when everyone else does. You'll know you're in the centre because you can see the castle on top of the hill, which is where I am now, sitting on a blistering bench, wondering – among other things – if cotton melts. Currently, it's certainly difficult to tell where thin, sodden shirt fabric ends and wet skin begins.

To be fair the views from up here really are quite magnificent, and while the blindingly white castle itself promises the dubious lure of a Furniture Museum, the well-kept grounds, walls and battlements are a delight. They shine in a Disney-like fashion, with apertures and balconies where princesses should swoon; all they lack is a prince plighting his troth from below with a boombox above his head like John Cusack in *Say Anything*.

The castle occupies the whole of a rocky hill above the river, a foursquare building with distinctive turrets that's existed in some form or other for a thousand years. The whole of Bratislava spreads out below, and much of the country too, for this is the rather pretty but unsung capital of Slovakia – a city of half a million in a total population of just five million, landlocked in a tight squeeze by Austria, Poland, Hungary, Ukraine and the Czech Republic.

Known for centuries by its German name, Pressburg, Bratislava has the usual list of historical Hapsburg, Hungarian and German comings and goings on its CV and was a thriving multi-ethnic city up until the Second World War. During and after that was the usual terrible tale of expulsions, death-camp deportations and forced evacuations, leaving a largely homogenous Slovak population that was later at the forefront of the anti-Soviet 'Velvet Divorce' that saw Czechoslovakia split into two in 1993. Nowadays Bratislava is considered to be resolutely Slovak in character and if you're not sure what that means, or says about the local population, consider the cycling and pedestrian bridge constructed near the capital back in 2012.

The local authorities decided to hold an online vote to decide on an official name – and yes, it was blindingly obvious to everyone except the authorities that this was never going to go well. The officials deliberated in committees, asked experts and consulted stakeholders, before proposing their own choice of the Freedom Cycling Bridge, since it crossed the Morava River to connect Slovakia with Austria – an escape route many had tried and failed to complete in Communist times. The sardonic locals, though, were having none of it. After all, being told what to vote for was what they had a revolution about. The overwhelming public write-in choice was the Chuck Norris Bridge, with the tough-guy film actor a byword in Slovakia for over-the-top macho jokes. Even today, try as they might, the council can't get anyone to call it the Freedom Cycling Bridge.

So the locals are funny – ha-ha, not peculiar – and the city centre is undeniably cute, with its narrow pedestrian streets, candy-coloured houses and manicured medieval air. It's probably the one European capital you could get around entirely in a day as almost everything of historic interest is tucked into the dinky old town underneath the castle. From my current perch I can see the wide Danube and the long concrete bridge I came over on the bus, known locally – there they go again – as the UFO bridge, on account of its saucer-shaped observation deck and restaurant-bar. I idly Google the top-deck restaurant, whose tagline is "Watch. Taste. Groove," so if you're ever looking for some bangin' contemporary action, Daddio, this is the place. If that isn't enough enticement, then does the fact that it's the seventh largest hanging bridge in the world persuade you? Or that it's the world's longest bridge to have one pylon and one cable-stayed plane, none of which I understand even after reading it twice on Wikipedia.

I stagger back down the cobbles from the castle thinking I might look for a spot of lunch and, while the main old town streets are lined with handsome buildings with a regal air, they are also a bit Prague-y and Stag Party-y. It's not quite the full waaay-haay, watch the scooter, sorry pal, but Bratislava is definitely on the beer-tour circuit. There is the Loch Ness Scottish Pub next to the Dubliner Inn, for example, where red-faced English gentlemen are opining that "It's fookin' hot" and questioning the whereabouts of "Soft lad with the beers". Tattoos – and I don't mean to be snobby, but on the forehead? – are very much *à la mode*, and there is much questioning of "Who the fook are you?" at passing strangers. These chaps – fine specimens all, my country should be proud – are clear candidates for pole-dancing and paintball, but have they not seen Eli Roth's seminal horror film *Hostel?* Basic story, college students are persuaded to visit Slovakia, drink copious amounts of cheap beer, enjoy the beauty and hospitality of Bratislava old town, get kidnapped, tortured and killed.

Look lads, if you've never done Film Studies, your problem.

I leave the pissed gents to it. They'll be fine. Probably.

A block back from the Danube are shaded riverside gardens, with a row of outdoor cafés and restaurants that appear to have a more genteel vibe. At the Restaurant Verne – what Jules is going to resist that? – the menu talks approvingly of "zander," which is a bony, mud-tasting river fish, and "beef tongue," which, well, you know. I think I'm going to give "bull's glands" and "fried cheese" a miss too. There's not a salad to be seen, though anyone with a desire for boiled, fried, braised, roasted or grilled cabbage would be well catered for. The waiter sees the sort of effete foreigner he's dealing with and talks me into trying the goulash and dumplings, much against my better judgement, the day now closing in on forty degrees. A hot, rich beef stew, laced with paprika and sour cream with a side order of starch, is clearly a mad choice, but it turns out to have surprisingly restorative powers. I laze in the shade and slowly recover, helped by tangy homemade lemonade that is sold by the litre. By the way, if you've ever wondered how much lemonade a human can drink in an hour, it's two litres.

It's very pleasant here in the dappled light. No one sings 'Wonderwall,' insults the waiter or spirits me away to a torture dungeon, always a bonus, and afterwards I walk slowly under spreading trees as far as the cathedral and contemplate an ice cream. Only contemplate. I've just had a summer injection of goulash and a bucketful of lemonade for Chrissake.

The cathedral, St Martin's, is curiously sited, right at the edge of the Old Town and below the castle, the two separated by a wide, roaring highway. There's no question that this is one of the oldest and most important churches in the country, where the Kings of Hungary were crowned for almost two hundred years. Yet here it stands, in an open courtyard, nowhere near the centre of town and just metres from concrete walls, flyovers and non-stop traffic. The answer to the puzzle is depressingly familiar. The cathedral – like all cathedrals – was of course once at the heart of Bratislava, built into the city's defensive walls and adjacent to a small but thriving Jewish old-town quarter. None of this mattered very much to Bratislava's Communist-era urban planners who swept away the ancient housing, synagogue and medieval walls so that they could build a highway leading to a new flagship river crossing – yes indeed, the UFO bridge.

From the marooned cathedral I circle back through town slowly, looking at this and that – "this" being the Old Town Hall, where a perspiring pianist is picking out a desultory tune in the attractive courtyard; and "that" being a very odd bronze sculpture set into the pavement of a smiling man peeping out of a manhole at up-skirt level. Cumil the Peeper is what the statue is called. That's not creepy at all is it?

There's plenty more in this vein – historic buildings, hidden stories, idiosyncratic sculptures, gushing fountains, pavement cafés. Like Prague, there's a fascinating city here itching to escape, once you get beyond the cheap beer and bars and dodgy town planning. Like Prague, it's just too hot. Eventually, I fetch up at the tourist office, where fate yet again does its thing.

Have you noticed that some of the best experiences you have on a trip or holiday are often those unexpected, serendipitous occasions when you just happen upon something? A wedding party you somehow get invited to; a chance glimpse of a hidden beach; an impromptu street concert? Those are the memories you take away and treasure – the things that mean more because you never expected them in the first place; the experiences you never even knew you could have, until they fell into your sizzling, sweaty, sun-baked lap.

The leaflet promises "Authentic Slovakia" and while I regard the word authentic with a certain amount of suspicion when it comes to travelling, I'm assured by the tourist office assistant that this is the real deal. The tour starts shortly and the reason I'm prepared to give it a go – sight unseen – is that it promises an in-depth investigation of Bratislava's Communist-era sights and attractions, such as the abandoned cigarette factory, the main Trades Union HQ and the Soviet-built TV transmitter building. And it does all this while driving you around in a chunky vintage Czechoslovak Škoda, one of those for-the-masses Eastern European classic vehicles where seatbelts and windows that opened were considered bourgeois luxuries. If that doesn't get your juices flowing, you have no soul.

I am directed around the corner to Slovak National Uprising Square, which is certainly a promising name for the start of a Communist tour. It's even more of a mouthful in Slovak – Námestie Slovenského Národného Povstania, dedicated to the armed insurrection of August 1944 against the Nazi invaders – though thankfully most locals settle for calling it Námestie SNP. This is where tour leader Juro – with a Y, Yuro (or George) – is waiting. Juro has good news and bad news, which would we like first?

"The good news is that we are going to go where normal tourists never go. To some places like Petržalka."

The Bratislava Bronx! Juro has no idea I'm a veteran of Petržalka. I should be leading this tour. It's bus number eighty Juro, I know all about it.

"The bad news today is that we don't have a Škoda. It's broken. Is that, how you say, ironic? But instead we are going in this green Volkswagen T4 minivan, which is still very uncomfortable."

I like Juro.

We drive off, on our way to the first stop, with Juro providing a deft running commentary that is basically news to the half a dozen of us on this trip. I know the basics – post-war reconstruction under Communism, Czechoslovakia, Iron Curtain, Velvet Revolution, a nation split in two, Czech Republic and Slovakia – but little of the social aspects of life here during those times. Juro and his family actually lived it. He grew up in the shadow of momentous political and economic changes, just thirty years ago, while we – from Britain, America and elsewhere – only saw it on TV. His country, Slovakia, only dates as an independent state from 1993; his experience of history is first-hand.

We bounce through town in the noisy Volkswagen, Juro pointing out bullet-marked buildings, neglected, weed-ridden 1970s plazas and a retro inverted pyramid building that resembles something out of *Futurama* and turns out to be the old, state-owned Slovak Radio HQ.

The stories aren't always as straightforward as they might seem. It's easy to think black and white, heroes and villains, Communism versus the West, but at the hilltop monument of Slavín we're invited to reflect upon the Soviet liberation of Bratislava in 1945. Almost seven thousand Soviet soldiers died retaking this city from the Nazis, their names etched on sheer reflective walls. Over eight million Soviet soldiers in all died during the Second World War (plus another twenty million citizens), which single fact informs much of contemporary Russian suspicion of the West. Here, as at so many similar battle sites and memorials, heroic friezes tell the story of partisan struggle, reprisals, invasion and eventual victory. We take a slow walk around the grandiose, sobering site, peer out over the city from the sweeping granite terrace and admire the mighty central obelisk topped by a triumphant soldier.

"Of course, we don't forget this" says Juro, but for his parent's generation – I guess Juro is in his late twenties – liberation didn't necessarily mean freedom. He points out the Christian cross that stands on the site now – "Absolutely impossible before 1989, because the Communists wanted to suppress religious tendencies." On the way out, Juro pulls the van into a parking bay in among the wealthy enclave of villas that lies just downhill from the monument.

"This is where the leaders, the Party bosses, the ambassadors all lived when I was growing up. People like us couldn't come up here."

Next up is a stunning viewpoint overlooking the River Danube, sited at the otherwise rather unprepossessing Hotel Bôrik, a Soviet-era hotel largely used for summits and conferences. In places the river marks the border with Austria and Hungary. In Communist times it was delineated by a hard 'wall' of barbed wire and concrete bunkers, and over four hundred people were shot and killed trying to escape to the West. Its location makes the hotel a place of some symbolism, even today, and it was often used to host the high and mighty; Brezhnev, Gorbachev, Yeltsin, Putin, Thatcher, Carter, Mitterrand, even the Queen, all stayed here at some point. Not at the same time, that would be the world's worst dinner party, and Putin would just keep taking his top off anyway and arm-wrestling Prince Phillip.

Juro explains all this while setting up a line of soft-drink bottles, which he then invites us to try.

"This is Kofola," says Juro. "Communist Coca-Cola. Made by a scientist who never tasted Coca-Cola."

I have a swig or two while looking out over the glinting Danube. It's not too bad – the right sort of colour and kind of fruity and herby – but Kofola doesn't taste anything like Coke, even if you squint into the sun and suspend your disbelief. It's nowhere near as sweet for a start and tastes almost homemade, which is not bad for something engineered by a scientist. It was invented in the 1950s, when Western goods were restricted and expensive to buy, and was cleverly marketed as an alternative to Coke, not a local rip-off, which would have fooled no one. Surprisingly perhaps, the drink has endured, possibly because Kofola never tried to be Coca-Cola, and it's still really popular in Slovakia and the Czech Republic today. It's a taste of the past that all sides can get nostalgic about.

"And now," says Juro with a flourish, "best of all, we are going to visit the largest housing estate in Europe."

Be still my beating heart. It's time for Petržalka.

Bless Juro for that "best of all," by the way. It's the sort of announcement that would get you thrown out of most Tour Guide Guilds ("Aafter we leave Buckingham Palace, best of all we are going to Tottenham,") but Juro is nothing if not sincere. He isn't showing us these prosaic sights to mock them or send them up; this isn't dark tourism, like visits to the Viet Cong tunnels or Chernobyl, presented as entertainment. Juro is a young man from a young country, genuinely conflicted about the recent past and willing to talk to strangers about awkward subjects. Communism marked his family's past, but not everything in that past was bad, wrong or mistaken.

During the Second World War, Bratislava was fought over, occupied, bombed and liberated. Imagine how that worked out for the city's inhabitants. Later, as people abandoned the rural villages of the East for work in the cities, a huge reconstruction programme took place on appropriated land across the river from the Old Town. With Communist zeal and efficiency, hundreds of prefab concrete tower-blocks were erected to house a population that eventually rose to over a hundred and twenty thousand. Juro wants to show us where most local residents call home, away from the tourist sights in the Old Town, and drives us across the UFO bridge – actually the Slovak National Uprising Bridge – and into the heart of Petržalka.

It's immense – the largest housing estate of its kind in Europe when it was built and still probably the most densely populated district in Central Europe. These were low-cost, quick-build constructions known as *paneláky*, or panel houses, all erected in a utilitarian, one-size-fits-all style, marching out away from the river in rows, squares and blocks as far as the eye can see. It might not have been pretty, but it was the kind of solution to a problem – the lack of decent housing – that could be imposed by a central command-and-control government. Everyone got a place to live, somewhere to call home, a reasonable level of security.

Juro is keen that we understand all this, and also that – whatever the system – people will find a way to live ordinary lives. We stop by an enormous lake, surrounded by trees and forest walks, and with grassy lawns and bathing areas.

"This was actually a gravel pit," says Juro. "It's where the raw material came from to build the estate. It's beautiful now."

Is this tour a holiday in other people's misery? Gravel pits, housing estates, Communist oppression – it would be easy to think that we're being asked to judge. But Juro doesn't have an edge, and if you're from Britain or the United States you've seen much worse housing projects than these, even if not in real life. They appear on the news, where seriously bad things happen, and yet for decades we were asked to believe that living and working for the all-seeing state and not having a meaningful democratic vote was somehow worse. It was worse to live here in the East than on a sink estate in London or New York, riddled with crime and drugs, because once every four or five years in the West you could, if you could be bothered or were even enfranchised, put a cross on a piece of paper.

I genuinely don't know. What's clear, though, after a short drive around, is that Petržalka was never really the Bratislava Bronx after all and never required gentrification. There's no stigma in having an apartment here. It is surprisingly green, laid out with parks and playgrounds, paths and bike lanes, and has always been considered a decent place to live. Outside observers might think it monolithic, sprawling, unlovely; residents just think of it as home. And over the years, especially since independence, a new feeling has taken hold as the locals have painted the exteriors of the once-uniform grey apartment blocks. Clubbing together in local councils and forums, the people who live here decided to change their environment.

Juro drives us around street after street where geometric shapes, outlines and colour bands have been applied to whole buildings, and the effect is mesmerising – harmonious ranks of colour-swatched towers in graded hues, like a giant Dulux paint catalogue. Thinking back to Vienna's Hundertwasserhaus, this is an entirely different use of line and colour – regimented, repetitive, straight-lined, reductive. But I think that the same spirit is at play, a very human desire to decorate, embellish and make personal a public living space. I've never seen a housing estate like it.

I am genuinely sorry when Juro delivers us back to Slovak National Uprising Square, after two eye-opening hours, rattling around Bratislava in an old Volkswagen van. This has been a great, and entirely unexpected, experience, as authentic as it comes. He's been warm, charming, welcoming and enlightening, and all for twenty-five euros. I don't feel that I know Slovakia now, but I do feel that I know a little bit more about it. And if you don't already want to adopt Juro, or at least wish him and his business well, wait until you hear what he says as I'm saying my goodbyes.

"After a tour," says Juro, "you should feel like you've been driving around with a bunch of friends. The passion for us is the history of Bratislava and getting to know other people from other countries. It's my dream job!"

And with that, he cranks up the old VW, crashes the gears and drives back off into authentic Slovakia.

Ljubljana

Intoxicated? The word did not express it by a mile. He was oiled, boiled, fried, plastered, whiffled, sozzled, and blotto. P.G. Wodehouse, *Meet Mr. Mulliner.*

A QUICK HOP from Bratislava back to Vienna and I'm on the through-train to Ljubljana, which I realise – when I examine the ticket closely – that I've been spelling incorrectly for years. It's only a small thing, but it bothers me that I have missed this until now. I get the tricky "lj" pronunciation – it's L-yoob-l-yarna – but until now have been steadfastly missing the second "j" and writing it as Ljubliana, with an "i" instead, which probably hasn't affected much the Slovenian national mood but annoys me now that I know about it. I resolve to do better by reciting "Luh-joob-luh-jana" every time I write it down in future. Which is going to be a lot in this chapter, so buckle up.

Luh-joob is the capital of Slovenia and if you can place it without looking at a map, you're doing better than most. There are mitigating factors at play if you went to school and studied geography in the years before 1989, after which the Berlin Wall fell and European map-makers said "Well thank you very much, got to draw all those bits again now." Once upon a time, taking a more or less straight line between Germany and Greece, there only used to be four countries: now there are ten, eleven if you recognise Kosovo, which Serbia doesn't but a hundred other countries do. Right there, in a nutshell, is why identifying Eastern European destinations is much harder than it used to be. It's all down to war, politics and national identity. Basically, yesterday I was in the bottom third of what used to be Czechoslovakia and today I'm going to the top bit of what used to be Yugoslavia. Find Venice and go east, if that helps? Are we oriented? Good stuff.

The gist of the day is that I'm on a Slovenian train riding south from Vienna and there are around six hours of slow cross-country travel ahead. To my mind, this is where European train travel excels.

You could fly this route in an hour, but once you add in travel to the airport, check-in times and luggage pick-up, there's no time saving (and it would be a whole lot more expensive). Plus, you don't see anything on the way, except the back of an aeroplane seat. Instead, I have the prospect of a leisurely journey through Austria and Slovenia, slipping into the sort of reverie that only a gently rocking train on a hot summer's day can provoke. Slumped back in a seat roomier than on any airline, gazing at the horizon, eyelids heavier by the minute, Europe both shrinks and expands in a half-asleep, half-awake moment that can stretch an hour or more. Stations and towns recede into the distance – places you'll likely never go, filled with people you'll likely never meet, though connected to you briefly as you pass through, tracing an imaginary line on a landscape you're both *in* and *of*, if just for a little while.

That's what train travel does for me, in any case. It slows me down and connects me to the great big map of Europe that I have in my head – the one that I'm lucky enough, as a European, to be able to cross at will by simply buying a ticket.

After a run of sleek intercity trains, I'm delighted to find that today I've got one of those enclosed, six-seater Agatha Christie-style carriages. Enter through a sliding door from the train corridor, three seats opposite each other, luggage racks towering overhead – the sort of old-school compartments you used to get in Europe, full of chain-smoking widows dressed head-to-toe in black, heavily armed soldiers on leave and market-traders with oversized candy-stripe bags full of small live animals. They're a real throwback– part of the romance of European train travel – but rife with danger. Trying to get in one of these carriages with a backpack when fully occupied is the sort of test they should give potential Foreign Office diplomats. If you can manage it without standing on a chicken or sitting in someone's lunch you get a plum posting in Paris; dare to move a widow's trunk a centimetre or two and it's Uzbekistan.

All the seats in my compartment are reserved, with a little ticket sticking out of each headrest, and there's the usual nervousness as we tick closer to departure time. Will they, won't they? Thrillingly, as the train moves off, apart from me the rest are no-shows. Woo-hoo, I get a window seat! Plus, I won't be murdered en route by a mysterious arms dealer with a twirly moustache.

The window seat is important because while the whole route today promises to be very scenic, the early section between Vienna and Graz follows the historic Semmering Railway, which is one of the most spectacular of all European rail routes. Built in the 1850s, it's considered the first true mountain railway – forty kilometres of extreme engineering involving fourteen tunnels, sixteen viaducts and over a hundred bridges, all built by hand.

We start handsomely enough among sunflower fields and pine-clad valleys, but after the station of Wiener Neustadt the train begins to make slow and steep curves up into the Austrian Alps, looping ever higher over double-decker bridges until crossing the Semmering Pass at nine hundred and eighty-five metres. It's never quite breathtaking – in the oh-my-god-we're-going-to-die sense – but it is a relentless reeling-in of slopes, cliffs, valleys and peaks as the train inches ever further into the mountains. The pass was once the highest place in the world you could reach by public railway, and the route has been in continuous operation ever since the track was first constructed. Between the two stations at either end – and could names be any more throat-clearingly magnificent than Gloggnitz and Mürzzuschlag? – it's only actually twenty-one kilometres, so the train travels double the distance to manage the huge difference in altitude.

I'm always astounded by feats of engineering such as this. The scale of ambition is overwhelming. Who looks at a mountain – an actual alp – and thinks "You know what, I could run a railway over that"? A Venetian-Albanian engineer called Carl Ritter von

Ghega is who, and in the 1850s remember, so that when Carl drew up his planned railway and realised he was going to need fourteen tunnels, that didn't give him pause for thought either. "Tunnels, schmunnels. We'll just dig through with picks and shovels" – I'm imagining Carl on a chaise-longue in a smoking jacket languidly dictating instructions to a long-suffering assistant who hasn't yet dared tell him they're also going to need sixteen viaducts. As I say, hard for a non-engineer to comprehend, though perhaps only the same as presenting an engineer with a sheaf of blank paper and asking them to write a travel book. They throw up their hands in horror and say, "A book, how on earth is that possible?" and I say "Book, schmook, we'll just throw fifty thousand words together, it'll be grand."

After the glories of the Semmering the train trundles on past Graz, Austria's second largest city, where quite a few more passengers pile on. My old InterRail pass – the one that kick-started this summer's trip – tells me that I have been to Graz before, but the same cloudy veil descends when I try to dredge up memories. Perhaps that's because, according to the pass, all I did was change trains on the same day for the eastern Austrian town of Gleisdorf (population, ten thousand, twinned with Nagykanizsa in Hungary), where I spent a baffling three nights. Not so much OBT (off-the-beaten-track) as WTF for a teenager with free travel anywhere in Europe. You might also ask why, later, I apparently passed through Rotterdam (cool buildings, hip culture and nightlife) for the chance to stay two nights in the Dutch town of Zaltbommel (notable resident, Marigje Arriens,

109

sixteenth-century Dutch witch)? On reflection, there are straightforward explanations – I was accepting invitations to go and visit people I'd met on the Swiss Alps workcamp, and if travel is about anything it's about flexible adaptation and serendipitous encounters, even in the arse-ends of Austria and the Netherlands. So while the decades have dulled the names and faces of my erstwhile dynamite-blasting, path-building buddies, I salute you Graz, Gleisdorf and Zaltbommel – places I have still visited more times (three) than India, Mexico and Russia combined (zero).

To be fair, had I known in advance about Graz's Key and Lock Museum – "the largest of its kind in the world" – you don't say – I might have arranged a stopover for today, but it's Luhjoob or bust. I stay put in my cosy six-seater compartment, which is promptly invaded by three middle-aged men carrying plastic bags that clink and chink as they arrange themselves in a noisy configuration by the door.

They are back-slappingly loud, leaning across to pummel each other on the knee and shoulder at intervals. Jokes – I assume they are jokes – are told and roars of laughter turn into actual heaves and sobs of monumental mirth. Every conversation opener is started at the volume of a pensioner's telly and then cranked up further as if broadcasting to Mars. Drinks are passed between each of them and downed quickly, with a hit rate of liquid to mouth of, I'd say, about eighty percent, with the other twenty moistening trouser legs, groins and carriage seats. They are, in short, what the Irish would call ossified, as well as fluthered, scuttered, banjoed, bolloxed, steaming, stocious,

110

elephants, langers and locked (the Irish do "drunk" words like the Inuit describe snow, with inventive and prolific variety). Given the clinking and chinking from the plastic bags, the trollied trio are also in possession of stuff that can only get them even more gargled, monkied and mullered than they already are.

On occasions like this, the trick is not to catch anyone's eye. The last thing I want is to be on the receiving end of any generous Slavic hospitality and pressed into joining in the drinking of small bottles of an unidentifiable white liquid with cans-of-beer chasers. In truth, though, they are oblivious that there is anyone else in the carriage.

They're not Austrian, because what they're speaking doesn't sound like German, but that's all I know. Slovenian? Possibly. It would be a good guess, but I refer you to the above problem of knowing what is where in Europe since the 1990s. Slovenian – and you'll just have to trust Google at this point – is spoken by only two million people but, get this, there are fifty different dialects. Sometimes dialects can be so different from one another, that it is hard for people from neighbouring parts of Slovenia to understand each other. Which perhaps explains the often indignant shouting that is going on in front of me, as Chap A and Chap B fail to appreciate the finer points of Chap C's humorous anecdote about the Orthodox priest, the donkey and the wetsuit.

The atmosphere is raucous but never offensive – these guys are *gone* – but my lazy journey is interrupted. They are not bothering me at all, other than the shouting and drinking, but the spell is broken. I can't zone out and idle away the hours when

111

Slovenian knock-knock jokes are being deconstructed at a thousand decibels by people from the next village who can't understand each other. Also, not to put too fine a point on it, it smells in here. The sun is pouring into the carriage – it's yet another ridiculously hot day – heating up our little party, and the alcohol fumes are rising. The window doesn't open – you have to go out into the corridor for any fresh air – and the aroma of Drunk-as-Skunk ("For Men. Slovenian Men.") hangs heavily in the air.

I grab my pack, squeeze past them at the door – I swear no one even notices – and sway down the corridor to the first window I can open. We clackety-clack on through rolling pastures and alpine villages, as I rest my forehead on the cool glass on this side of the train, but that soon loses its appeal as the train jerks and lurches its way out of Austria and into Slovenia.

What I need is sanctuary and I find it in the dining car, two carriages further down. The air-conditioned dining car, I might add. It's unfathomably deserted – cool air plays down the carriage, the tables are laid with tablecloths, the cushioned seats are springy, and there's waiter-service food and drink available, yet I am the only person in here. No matter, their loss, let's have a look at this menu.

There's a printed card with the menu in Slovenian and English, though that isn't as helpful as it sounds. The Slovenian side describes each item in loving detail in forty or fifty words, perhaps describing the side of the valley on which the cossetted pig was raised and itemising the kind treatment it received, while

112

the English side simply says "Sausage." It's much the same with "Soup" and "Fruit," but I'm hungry so soup, sausage and fruit it is.

The waiter eventually arrives – you can tell his heart isn't in it, I suspect I woke him up – and there is a fair amount of pointing (me) and jotting down screeds of notes and impenetrable symbols (him). What can he possibly be writing? It's soup, sausage and fruit, three dishes and four syllables, for the one and only customer. He finally seems satisfied and closes his pad with a flourish. I should think the notes say "Foreign, poss. English? Soup AND sausage!! Fruit – check tin OK?"

"Soup" turns out to be beef-and-noodle, a thin stock bobbing with bits of unidentifiable meat and sliced vegetables. From the lengthy clattering in the galley at the end of the dining car, I take it that this has been prepared on board – by the waiter, who seems to be doubling up as chef. It's not like he's overworked but, to be fair to him, there is no giveaway ping from a microwave and it's very tasty.

Next up is "Sausage" and here the English-language side of the menu has not let me down in the slightest. I am presented with a single, curving sausage. A fat, grilled, bratwurst-style sausage, but a single sausage nonetheless, served with a bread roll and a small dish of mustard. I do admire a straight-talking menu – in a fancy English restaurant this would be a "A singularity of mechanically recovered pork sausage accompanied by an oven-warmed baker's roll and mustard-seed condiment." I do also love a sausage, so this is another excellent choice and so far it's

Slovenian Dining Car 1, Drinkers' Carriage 0. In fact, I'm now even more mystified as to why I'm the only customer. Does no one realise that sausages are to be had?

And so to dessert, or "Fruit", which is – I called it – a glass dish of tinned fruit and squirty cream, which takes me right back to school dinners in the canteen. In fact, add chips to the sausage and pretty much the entire meal is a throwback to my junior school days, only I haven't had to eat in constant fear of a wedgie or worse from the rough boys with dropped voices and razored hair. School lunch was the time when swots like me were most at risk from unwanted aggravation – the teachers had retreated to the staffroom for cigarettes, whisky chasers and a snooze, leaving the way clear for the persecution of anyone unwise enough to come to school in a tie and blazer.

Indeed, the school dinner queue is where I first learned the subtle art of not catching anyone's eye. It was a critical survival skill. Earlier, in the carriage, the worst that could have happened was a bout of enforced alcohol poisoning, rapid liver destruction and death. At school, by attracting the wrong type of attention, I could have been pinned down on the dining table, my poetry homework exhumed from my bag and read out loud to a merciless crowd, underpants twanged and rice pudding applied to my hair. Much, much worse than a liquid death on the Ljubljana express.

I sit nursing a black coffee or two, dozing in the fierce sunshine, as the train emerges from the Slovenian hills before a final run alongside a deep green river that flows right into the centre of Ljubljana. Here we are, Luh-joob at last – and bang on time by the way, even after six hours on super-heated rails in baking temperatures.

This punctuality is not a given if you're used to rail travel in the UK, where the "wrong kind of leaves on the line" in autumn (genuine excuse) or a drop in temperature in winter of a couple of degrees leads to weeks of chaos, trains abandoned between stations, commuters storming ticket offices and questions in Parliament. Alternatively, if the temperature climbs above twenty-seven degrees in Britain – and that's not *that* hot – the train network goes all *Mad Max* as the concrete rail sleepers start to stress and crack, the steel rails buckle and feral junkie warlords fight it out at Orpington Junction. The cunning Europeans, it seems, use wooden sleepers instead of concrete (to allow for heat expansion) and stress their steel at a higher temperature range, which is why I'm gliding into Ljubljana at bang on the arrival time. And am not stranded at the Slovenian equivalent of Watford because of the "wrong kind of sun."

Outside the Luh-joob train station concourse it's eye-poppingly, blisteringly hot, the tarmac searing the soles of my canvas shoes. I can feel the heat reflected off the station building walls and there isn't a hint of a breeze – just the immediate presence of the sun, which feels as if it's been yanked ninety-three million miles from its mooring and stationed about two metres directly above my head. Luckily, the place I'm staying in is just a few minutes' walk away and surprisingly easy to find, because all

I have to do is walk in the general direction indicated by my phone and look for the building that resembles a prison.

The neighbourhood, known as Metelkova, was once the site of a sprawling army barracks that was abandoned in the 1990s after the break-up of Yugoslavia. Artists moved in ("Rent-free buildings! Walls we can paint on!") and set up workshops, studios and galleries, while the old military prison eventually became the Hostel Celica ("Surrender and spend a night behind bars,") still with its cells and barred windows but now transformed into something they call an art hostel. At first sight, it looks like all they've done is let loose some free-range graffiti artists into the surrounding high-walled yards and painted the exterior in clashing pastel colours. But inside, as I ease my backpack off, it's clear that this is a very cool conversion, from the garden courtyard hung with hammocks to the inventive graphics and murals on the walls.

There are dorm beds in the attic but I'm too old to sleep in a room full of backpackers. Besides, my Olympic-level snoring will only keep them awake, poor loves. Instead I've booked one of the twenty original cells, each styled by an international artist or designer and no two the same. We're talking serious quality here – one cell has a glazed floor covering sixteen Anthony Gormley statuettes; another has a wall etched with a blue acrylic-paint mural by a notable Russian set designer. Others use handcrafted or found objects to tell a story or illustrate a theme, so there's upcycled furniture, recycled barracks bricks, painted wood, vintage metal beds and even framed notes from ex-prisoners.

My gaff, Cell 114, has two raised wooden cots in a light-filled room that's more vertical than horizontal, girded by a strip of arty photos of Slovenia. It's cool and white, and minimally furnished with a boxy pine seating area and a few hooks for clothes. The inner door is a high metal grille that opens and closes with an authentic-sounding clang. If they ever build a prison for hipsters – to house the worst of the wax-moustachioed, craft-beer-brewing, kombucha-drinking, bicycle-riding, avocado-toasting, plaid-scarf-wearing offenders – this is what it will look like. "Take him down," the judge will say, "shave off his beard" – scuffles in the dock, cries of "Nno, not the beard!" – "and put him in the cell with the window in the shape of a vulva that symbolises a rebirth of an old object into a new life."

After six hours on a train, I could happily do nothing except lie on my artfully designed bunk until it's artisan-beer-time downstairs in the bar. But years as a travel guidebook writer have ruined me, or at least made holidays difficult to navigate. I usually arrive with a run-down of things to see and do, a hit-list of hotels and a roster of restaurants to investigate. Even when I'm Holiday Guy and my time's my own, I still always feel like there's something I should be attending to – somewhere I should be checking out – even when the only sensible thing to do is lie down in a cool white room for an hour or two. As with most travel-writing gigs, I'm only here for a short time – less than a day in fact – and while I don't have any bus timetables to copy down or art galleries to canter through, I do want to feel as if I've seen something of Ljubljana other than Hipster Hostel Cell Block H.

Normal people – even hipster backpackers – will be chilling in a hammock downstairs and contemplating a cocktail made by an extravagantly tattooed Slovenian bartender. I'm not normal. Although a hammock and a cocktail would be most welcome, I'm basically straining at the leash to go and see something historic and cultural.

I was going to say that the city centre is just ten minutes' walk away, but having walked into it I am revising my opinion. The ten minutes bit is fine, but while this might be a capital it's no city; rather a mere town – population, just a quarter of a million – and it's immediately and utterly delightful. I hit the narrow River Ljubljanica, which is criss-crossed by a number of handsome bridges and lined with dozens of outdoor cafés. It's traffic-free, not a car in sight – nor indeed, it seems, allowed. Is there a prettier urban riverside in Europe? I'm not sure there is. There are willow-draped banks, shady walks and market stalls, with spires and balconied buildings rising high above, yet if it's touristy it's only so in the sense that there are tourists here, myself included. But the overwhelming feel is of a town – sorry, city – that knows the value of taking time out at some point during the day. Of banishing vehicles, giving the streets back to humans, switching the phone ringer to silent, ignoring work emails and sitting down in the riverside shade with a beer or a coffee.

I get that I'm in the historic old town, and that not all of Ljubljana is like this, but there's something laidback and appealing about all this being the heart of a working capital city. I would not choose to sit in an outdoor café on Leicester Square

– not without my hand on my wallet and ammunition for my busker-repelling AK47 – but I am sorely tempted to give into temptation, lounge in the first riverside seat I can find and summon up the Slovenian for "beer". (If you've been paying attention since Prague, it will come as little surprise that it's *pivo*.)

However, right now I'm aiming for the fairytale castle overlooking this pint-sized capital, high on the hill above the river. It looks the part – walls, ramparts, maidens dangling their hair from the towers – and is the obvious place to go for a literal overview of Ljubljana. From down by the river it seems ridiculously close, but that's because the hill it's on is ridiculously steep. You might be tempted to walk up – there's a signposted path – but have I mentioned the temperature? I think I may have touched upon it. Luckily, there is a funicular and of all the types of railway, the funicular is best. It's short, it's steep, it does the job, and in Ljubljana it does the job for four euros return. Why wouldn't you?

It takes a few minutes to slide up the hill through the trees, climbing ever higher above the red roofs of Ljubljana. At the top the funicular disappears into the bowels of the castle, where we're disgorged before being funnelled out, along and up corridors and staircases to emerge into the massive castle courtyard. It's impressive in its way – there's been a fortification here for over nine hundred years – but it's pretty clear that restorations and renovations have robbed the castle of much of its character. It may represent centuries of Slovenian history but it's been over-prettified, and it doesn't help that it's marketed as a cultural and entertainment venue. I see signs for – count them – a jazz club, puppetry museum, history exhibit, theatre, video room, two restaurants and a café, while glass walls, fancy decking, landscaped walkways and parasols give it the air of an Ibiza beach club. Not my kind of history, I have to say, though as I only came up here for the view I'm happy enough on the terrace you can access for free from the courtyard. I can just about make out the river and outdoor market between the tightly packed buildings way down below, and then sweep my eyes across the sloping roofs and pointy spires to the distant mountains. There will be an even better view from the dinky clocktower across the courtyard, but that means buying a ten-euro ticket for everything else in the castle and I'm just not in the mood.

In fact, by now, I've had enough. At the end of this long, ludicrously hot day, Travel Writer Guy has officially resigned and handed over the reins to Holiday Guy, with one simple multi-part instruction: go back to the hostel, have a cold shower, drink beer, find food. Holiday Guy – it's me everyone, are you getting that it's me? – manages the first three of these things, no problem, but is daunted by the prospect of number four if it means walking back into the centre again to look for a restaurant. It's now about seven pm but is no cooler. I suspect that Venus – hottest planet in the solar system, and that's science – has also been shunted across to double-up with the sun directly over Ljubljana.

However, what works in Vienna also works here. I ask about a nearby place to eat at the hostel reception and they recommend

I simply go around the corner to the local grill-house. "It's Serbian," they say, as if that should explain something.

In front of a nondescript apartment building a few plastic tables occupy a tree-shaded yard, heady with the oily scent of charcoal. Tiny birds hop from chair to chair, while assorted young men hover in corners of the yard throwing peanuts at the birds. If I hadn't been told it was a restaurant, I wouldn't necessarily recognise it as one, and I'm still not entirely sure as I pull up a seat.

A young man peels himself away from his mates and produces a menu based on what I am now beginning to recognise as the Standard Slovenian Model; ie, an impenetrable Slavic essay on one side and some random English words on the other. After a bit of pointing I order the "Mix grill," because that seems to be the done thing and it makes the waiter happy, and then I sit back drinking a red wine so cheeky and fresh it's basically telling me jokes and slapping my thighs.

When it arrives on a Desperate-Dan-sized platter, the "Mix grill" turns out to be both dinner and Serbian endurance and initiation ceremony. There are endless little aromatic minced beef-and-pork kebabs, known as *cevapi*, each about the size of a cigar – you'd think half a dozen of this would be sufficient for one, but you'd be wrong. A veritable cartwheel of a cheese-stuffed burger-type thing takes up another part of the platter, and just for good measure there are half a dozen spicy sausages that are a cross between a *chorizo* and a hot dog, oozing a slick of paprika oil. Everything is tinged with a smoky, slightly charred

121

flavour that says a really hot grill has been involved. There are French fries – really good French fries – and a thick, ochre-coloured, pepper relish with a throaty, garlicky kick. If you're wondering about the vegetables, good luck with that, though there is a creamy slaw and, just in case I haven't got enough starch and carbs, several rounds of chewy flat bread that have possibly been deep-fried or at least waved over the fryer.

It's impossibly tasty and I dive in, to the obvious approval of the waiter's mates. They are standing half in, half out, of the restaurant doorway, smoking furiously as plates of food are carried past them. I suppose technically they are outside the restaurant and beyond the long arm of the smoking law, but then again, I am beginning to think that things like that don't count for very much in Slovenia. There's an ashtray on every table for example, and when after a while a kitchen hand comes out to take a break, he already has a lit cigarette in his mouth. Chef presumably is chain-smoking and lighting them from his grill, but a man who can wrestle such flavoursome taste from minced pork and beef is all right by me.

To finish, there's a little brass pot of muddy Serbian coffee, and more impertinent red wine that's now so impudent it's chucking my cheeks and ruffling my hair. The waiter takes away what's left – not much – and retreats to the doorway for more peanut-throwing. I have defeated the meal and, if I understand correctly, am now an honorary Serbian with all the rights and privileges that entails. The bill by the way, if you can call it a bill, comes to fifteen euros.

When I come to write the history of this trip, I shall reflect upon my first day in a country I've never visited before; on the prettiest little capital city imaginable; and on river walks and castle views. I'll recall the heat rising from the pavements and the cool walls of a hip hostel in an arty Slovenian neighbourhood.

But mostly I'll be thinking, "How and when am I going to Serbia, oh land of my fathers and prince of cuisines?"

Zagreb

He who dines on wine has water for breakfast. Croatian proverb.

THE TROUBLE WITH being an honorary Serbian by dint of diet is that you don't leap out of bed each morning with a merry cry, fully refreshed and raring to go. My night in the cell has been one of fevered dreams and food sweats, helped neither by the relentless heat nor by the lack of a curtain for the window – which I didn't notice until it got light at about four am and the local birds called an important meeting right outside. Tweeting and chirruping were definitely on the agenda; squawking was under Any Other Business as I recall. Sleep, in short, was not the main course in life's feast and the most nourishing, as the Bard claims. I'd say the little kebabs and red wine put paid to that.

At least today I don't have to get up for an early train. I'm bound for Zagreb and Croatia on the 14.45, which gives me plenty of time to recover, and I vow to do it on the River Ljubljanica. I spotted several low-slung, flat-bottomed cruise boats yesterday chugging under the bridges in town and the thought of slumping back on a padded seat in a river breeze appeals mightily. There's something about a boat trip that always revives the spirits and even if I can't embrace the elements from the bow, Titanic style, I can attempt to shake off what uncharitable observers might think of as a hangover.

A hipster breakfast downstairs in the hostel café also does much to perk me up – there's crushed avocado, thinly sliced cheese, thick yoghurt, honey from a local bee-farm and homemade lemonade with fresh ginger and mint leaves. The zesty lemonade, in particular, has many of the properties of the pick-me-up beverage provided by the man-servant Jeeves to Bertie Wooster after a night on the tiles – for a moment it feels like someone is strolling down my throat with a lighted torch and then there are singing birds and dawning hope, and all seems right with the world. Naturally, the Serbian in me disapproves of all this wholefood goodness; I suspect I should be breaking my fast with tiny kebabs and a glass of Belgrade red. I hope my new people aren't watching.

The cruise boats line up under one of the central bridges, known as the Butchers' Bridge, which backs onto the market building and market square. There's something extremely striking – almost regal – about the market setting, the two-storey building curving along the river, with covered stalls spilling out across the square. This is a market worth coming back too, I feel. There are cafés too, but (*checks time, considers it briefly, thinks of consequences*) it's a bit early for a *pivo* and the boat is waiting.

Out we chug at a gentle pace under the Triple Bridge (an eye-catching three criss-cross pedestrian bridges in one, all highly confusing) and then slowly through the ornamented buildings that line either side of the river. From the water, it's obvious that there's a real harmony to this part of the city centre, with embankments, market buildings, bridges and thoroughfares all part of the same urban plan by an architect called Jože Plečnik, who re-shaped the city in the years between the two world wars. He gave his buildings and bridges Classical embellishments such as pillars, columns and pediments – and a full colonnade in the case of the impressive market. His inspiration was ancient Athens, or at least its meeting places, public spaces and civic architecture, and a slow drift downriver is the best way to appreciate the city as Plečnik envisaged it – a designed work of art.

We're so low in the water, I can almost trail my fingers in the ripples. The river looks pretty inviting for a city-centre waterway – sparkling and sun-dappled, not filled with abandoned supermarket trolleys – and we pass kayaks and stand-up paddleboarders and any number of dog-walkers, pram-pushers, sunbathers, picnickers and bench-kippers. The high embankments and elevated promenades give way to willow-draped riverside suburbs, where houses start to come with jetties and boat shacks instead of driveways. I'd say we're about twenty minutes out of downtown Ljubljana at this point, so this seems a pretty agreeable place to live all round. Jagged mountains loom tantalisingly on the near horizon. Mountains, I am delighted to learn, that are called the Julian Alps. Thank you, so kind. My mountains, as I shall now think of them.

The driver – boatman? captain? – eventually does a three-point turn and we slosh back towards the city centre, with a final flourish as we double-back under Ljubljana's most famous bridge. There's a rearing copper dragon on each corner of the

Zmajski Most – the Dragon Bridge – though I only get a glimpse from the river and need to walk around to see properly afterwards. It's the symbol of the city – there's a dragon on the Ljubljana coat-of-arms – probably adopted from the same martyred Roman officer, later Saint George, who pops up as patron saint of England, Catalunya, Ethiopia and the Republic of Georgia. You might ask, why Slovenia too? But it seems entirely probable that someone who could get lost between England and Spain ("Hang on, is this Georgia? Let me see that map again") would travel to Ethiopia via central Europe.

The river cruise has done the trick. I examine my psyche, flex the old neurons and breathe deeply, and decide on balance that I am restored to something approaching full fettle. I haven't mentioned today's heat – have you ever crouched down and opened an oven door too quickly, so that you think you have melted your eyes? – because even to acknowledge its existence is to threaten my hard-gained equilibrium. I intend to accept and transcend, much as a Buddhist would do if they found themselves tethered to a hot plate by accident.

Today's train ride should be a doddle, a lazy two-and-a-half-hour trundle along the river from Ljubljana to Zagreb, the capital of Croatia. I already have the ticket, courtesy of the saintly Man in Seat 61, whose train-travel website advised me that I could buy one for half-price by simply getting it the day before at Ljubljana train station. I snapped one up on arrival yesterday, which is why I'm now able to travel a hundred and sixty kilometres between two European capital cities for just nine euros. That's the price of a glass of wine in Paris, which means one of these things is very good value and the other very bad value, and I leave you to make the judgement.

I'm also promised a gorgeous, snaking ride along the River Sava all the way, but what The Man in Seat 61 can't legislate for is the other occupants of the railway carriage. It's another old-fashioned six-seater, fully occupied this time as I take the last seat by the sliding door, and just as the train starts to inch its way out of Ljubljana station the two passengers by the window – with the full agreement of the other three – pull down the sun-blind.

Now here's a tricky bit of train etiquette. I didn't get to vote – clearly foreign and disenfranchised – but if invited I would have given a rousing, Twelve-Angry-Men-style appeal to reason and decency and would, I'm sure, despite the language difficulties, have prevailed. The jury would be swayed and the blind would be up, the sun pouring in on six disparate passengers who have made an emotional journey and now share a common bond, and I'd be able to see the bloody river. But the blind is down, and clearly staying down, and the river is to remain un-seen. So every now and again I nip out to the carriage lobby and snap a pic or two through the train door of what looks like a rather breath-taking route, and then come back to my seat to harrumph and scowl for a bit. I agree that it is much cooler in our shaded compartment than it is in the furnace of a corridor or in front of the dazzling train-door window, but that is decidedly Not The Point. So the journey passes.

Zagreb turns out to be a magnificent-looking city at first sight, which for me this is. Even the station – especially the station – resembles a rather grand palace that would satisfy a Croatian prince, while several other buildings that stretch out down the central gardens very probably are palaces. So there's that, but there's also the hostel building where I'm staying, which is less like a palace and more like – well, ironically enough, given that I stayed in an actual prison last night, a prison. To be fair to the place, it's not shockingly shabby and it is cheerily and efficiently run. No one's being locked into solitary confinement or given mailbags to sew, at least not as far as I can see. But it's very definitely on the tired side of utilitarian, while I now expect art, avocado and artisan ale from my hostels.

My private, en-suite room with view looked and sounded a whole lot grander when I booked it online. Let's break down the 'balcony with garden view' for example. I'm a couple of storeys up and there are French windows, which open onto about six inches of a concrete ledge with only a rusty metal fence preventing a death-plunge. That would be the balcony then. There is a view of sorts and I suppose the hostel management could channel Basil Fawlty and ask what I was expecting to see from a Zagreb window – "Sydney Opera House, perhaps? The Hanging Gardens of Babylon? Herds of wildebeest sweeping majestically?" I look out instead over the "garden," which consists of a pot-holed concrete parking lot, several abandoned cars, a corrugated tin roof and an assortment of rusty, fractured drainpipes, not all of which appear to be up to the job of draining water.

The tiny en-suite bathroom is also a classic of its kind, with the toilet wedged up so hard against the shower door that it's impossible to conceive of using either in any kind of conventional way. There's no window and the room is tiled from floor to ceiling in a fairly random collection of designs, with any gaps and cracks filled with flaking concrete. It's disappointing but it's hard to be too judgmental, seeing as I have paid the princely sum of thirty-five euros for the night. Hell, I've stayed in *far* worse places than this, notably the backpacker guesthouses of Chungking Mansions in Hong Kong, where you can touch all four walls of your room, turn the light on and off and flush the toilet all without moving from your bed. Here in Zagreb I also have a window, which does not come as standard in Chungking – unlike tattoo parlours, cockroaches, pungent drains, labyrinthine corridors with trailing electrical cables and dripping water pipes, which do.

If there is a major disappointment though it's that there's no plug in the sink, which is unfortunate because I have earmarked Zagreb – halfway point in the journey – as the place to do my laundry. Even on a nine-day trip, I'm not carrying all the clothes I need, so this day was always going to come. But what I was banking on in my thirty-five-euro en-suite room was a fully functional sink. I'd have paid an extra euro for a plug, had that been an optional extra.

As any experienced traveller knows, a sink plug is the most crucial item for clothes-washing, because it means you stand a fighting chance of not over-burdening the drainage system and causing an international water-related incident. I have in the past, for example, flooded a bathroom floor in Dublin resulting in a ceiling leak below (very upsetting for the couple in bed apparently). It seems that you should not run the bath taps to soak your jeans, go and switch on the TV and get side-tracked by an episode of *Neighbours*. How was I supposed to know? I was also once on the end of a stern ticking-off in Portugal regarding sock-washing and a faulty overflow pipe, the proprietor having been under said pipe at quite the wrong moment. To be fair to him, as he stood at the door gesticulating furiously, you could see that he wasn't going to dry out any time soon.

As any experienced traveller also knows, you take a travel sink plug with you wherever you go, just in case. I have a little rubber, one-size-fits-all, plughole blocker. I never travel without it. Only – as I spread all my things out on the bed in an increasingly exasperated fashion – it appears that on this occasion I have. Got the warm fleece, for when it gets chilly – ha! I say – don't worry about that, but of the sink plug there is no sign. And as you know – given the prospect from the garden-view balcony – I already have no confidence in the local drainpipes.

The answer – useful travel tip – is a single sock stuffed in the plug-hole while I slosh and sluice in scalding water that has a worrying brown tinge. In place of detergent I am squeezing shampoo out of a little sachet into the sink, which produces such

131

an alarming volume of suds and bubbles that I could bathe a baby elephant. The sink fills and empties as I wring and rinse, and hard as I try I can't keep the water from flowing over the side. It's also become terrifyingly hot in the tiny bathroom – so hot that I am now stripped down to trunks only – and there's soon enough water on the few square inches of available floor that it's lapping around my toes and rising up the outside of the toilet bowl. The sweat pouring off me probably adds another inch to the level.

On will-sapping occasions like this, the trick is to get out before you're discovered. The knock on the door could come at any minute. I wring everything out as best I can, drape the now steaming clothes over chair and bedframe, throw on shorts and T-shirt and head out to investigate Zagreb. And in shock news, it turns out that while I've been inside creating the exact atmospheric and chemical conditions necessary for single-cell life to form, there's been a change in the weather.

The temperature has dropped from a sticky, steamy thirty-five degrees to a more manageable twenty-seven, but this hugely welcome relief is accompanied by a thunderstorm and torrential rain. For the first few minutes it's delightful, standing in the manicured central gardens of Zagreb, arms wide apart, feeling the breeze on my face and cooling drops on my head. For the first time since landing in Berlin, there's no oppressive, sledgehammer heat. The rain becomes more insistent but it's still enjoyable, wandering the gravel paths with a damp but not sweaty T-shirt. Then, with a single clap of almighty thunder, the sky scowls and someone turns on the jets.

I leg it to the first available bar through an unassuming doorway and spend the next couple of hours in the crumbling, tree-planted courtyard of the rather fine Bacchus Jazz Bar. Young men – who look exactly like you'd expect young men in an eastern European jazz bar to look – are reading poetry under the trees to Manic Pixie Dream Girls lounging on cushions. Sartre is doubtless being discussed. Irony-free black polo necks are definitely being worn. Every time the bar door opens, discordant sounds escape – possibly freestyle jazz of a rather extreme nature or perhaps the engineer banging his tools as he fixes the honking ventilation system. It's difficult to say. All this is very charming and adds greatly to the gaiety of nations. Always love a good jazz bar. If there's a downside it's that biting insects are out in force, sensing the change in the weather, but I apply a pint of feisty Croatian IPA beer which seems to keep them off.

The driving rain rather puts paid to any plans I have to mooch around Zagreb. I have a night here and then most of the day tomorrow before taking the overnight sleeper train to Zürich, but the next twenty-four hours settles into a pattern of scudding clouds, furiously dark skies and then rain of the sort that could float an ark. You can never quite predict it either, so a sortie from the jazz bar when the first deluge relents quickly turns into another dash for a sheltered doorway, and this continues for the duration of my stay.

This is a huge pity. It's my first time in Croatia and I've heard great things about Zagreb. Important since medieval times but pummelled by fire, plague and earthquakes over the centuries, and rebuilt handsomely since, it's got a nineteenth-century grandeur and a dynamic, twenty-first-century vibe. Since the late-1990s, after war and independence and especially in the last decade or so, Zagreb has found its feet as a pretty hip destination. Lonely Planet made it their number-one European city a few years back. Rough Guides call it a "collector's item for city connoisseurs." I should be cruising the upper and lower towns, attending gallery openings, browsing in Dolac market, tracking down the street murals and hanging out in hipster bars. I'd like to call in at the Museum of Broken Relationships – ain't that an alluring prospect? – and wander the Botanical Gardens. I should be sitting on benches in shaded squares, eavesdropping on students talking earnestly of subjects – bless them – that they don't know anything about. There's even a funicular railway – and you know how I feel about funiculars – that's claimed to be one of the shortest and steepest in the world. A quick, pointless train ride up an almost vertical hill – that's got my name all over it.

Sadly, I can't do any of these things. The rain is less in the manner of falling droplets and more in the way of a thundering waterfall. It simply pours out of the sky, pounding up from the pavements like those squirting jets in plazas through which children run. It does this for half an hour at a time or more and then reduces to a more manageable, regulation downpour. When it stops the city steams, and then with no warning the rain starts up again. There's no prospect of going anywhere without getting soaked to the skin – and let's not forget that the only clean clothes I have are very far from being dry. They are not even in the same postcode as being dry; they are currently dripping from a bedframe in the Hostel Steam N'Sluice while the manager bangs forlornly on the door and shouts imprecatory words about guests doing forbidden laundry in the rooms.

Between cloudbursts I do make it down the central gardens, through the main square and up as far as the twin-turreted cathedral. But while the city certainly makes a fleeting impression – grand and spacious, big statues, plenty of greenery – I don't get the chance to take it in, at least in any meaningful way. This was always going to be a brief stay, as with every destination on this trip, but dodging severe thunderstorms ultimately means spending time in one café after another until my next train. This is hardly a trial – Zagreb does coffee and cake with an almost Viennese skill and determination – but for a person itching to see "stuff" in a city he's never visited before, it takes some doing to sit and chill.

At some point during the next day, a couple of blocks over from the cathedral, I dive into a random place to escape yet another torrential downpour. The Sri Lankan Curry Bowl turns out to be a real find, a hole-in-the-wall restaurant on Zagreb's food alley run by two Sri Lankan brothers who fetched up here after a backpacking tour. The food is great – spicy fried rice, coconut curries, warm *dhal* soups, all served with a real charm and warmth. I've often considered that there is no rice dish that can't be improved by plonking a fried egg on it, and Sri Lanka agrees, so I sit here for an hour or two that turns into three and eat and drink happily while the heavens do their thing.

The alley is literally now a river, with the drains overwhelmed and water gushing past the raised deck of the café. One of the owners holds up the awning – bulging dangerously under the weight of collected rainfall – so that we can all continue our meals without it collapsing upon us. Occasional tourists splash past, having abandoned any efforts to hide from the rain, and eventually I'll have to join them, to work my way back towards the hostel to pick up my backpack and head for the station.

But for now the journey is halted, the trains and sightseeing on hold. I surrender to the swirling elements, sip yet more coffee under a pattering canopy and let Zagreb go.

Liechtenstein and Zürich

Everything about Liechtenstein is ridiculous. Bill Bryson, *Neither Here Nor There.*

ON THE FACE of it, taking the night train from Zagreb to Zürich seems both like an incredibly odd yet romantically adventurous thing to do – pick two random European cities beginning with "z" and travel between them on a rattling sleeper-train with all its period-piece connotations. Continental jewel thieves, arms dealers, eloping runaways, disgraced financiers, ambassadors of long-forgotten principalities and down-at-heel European nobility – all basically included in the ticket price.

It's an eight-hundred-kilometre, fifteen-hour trans-alpine route through Croatia, Slovenia and Austria that makes no geographical sense for anyone flying home from Milan in a few days, except that I have two very good reasons. First, tomorrow morning, just before Zürich, the train makes a stop at the Swiss station of Sargans, departure point for the short bus ride to Liechtenstein. It's the only time in the entire trip that I'm taking a bus instead of a train, but they're my rules and I'm going to allow it. Second, I plan to arrive in Milan in style on the final leg of my trip, which means crossing the Alps from Zürich via Chur on the glorious Bernina Express – arguably the finest of all European mountain railway journeys.

137

So to get me in place for Liechtenstein and the Bernina Express, the 18.38 Zagreb-Zürich sleeper it is.

If I'm expecting white-gloved attendants and a welcoming brass band at Zagreb station – and you know I am – then disappointment kicks in early. The train waiting for me on the platform doesn't look much like a palace of intrigue on wheels; more like it's just come off a shift hauling coal from a Croatian open-cast mine. It's better on inspection inside – basic but clean – but it is blisteringly hot now the rain has stopped and the temperature is starting to rise again. I make enquiries and the air-conditioned buffet car that I had been planning to spend the evening in, chatting to mysterious widows over caviar and champagne, turns out to be a figment of my over-heated imagination. The catering facilities consist of a lady with a tray of packaged croissants and instant coffee that can only be accessed at seven o'clock the following morning. The good news is I have a greasy cheese pie bought from the station kiosk, so at least that's dinner sorted.

As we pull out on time, I'm looking forward to the first leg of the journey in particular, because it's back along the river to Ljubljana – the beautiful route I was denied a view of yesterday in the whole Window Blind Incident. I make my way to my reserved compartment where it's disappointingly clear that gazing out at the rolling Balkan countryside is not an option this time either, since the cabins are already made up into beds. There's nowhere to sit and the windows are obscured by the foot-ends of the upper bunks. That puts paid to slouching in a seat for an hour or two, idly watching the world go by as the setting sun casts shadows on reflective rivers and picturesque valleys. Which leaves standing in the corridor, getting in the way of the conductor and attempting to translate the various warning signs – leaning out of the window, apparently not recommended; ditto opening the window and throwing things out of the window. Basically, don't touch the window. Which rather reduces the entertainment and intrigue possibilities on the Zürich express to zero. Poirot would probably be the one committing murder on this train, just to jolly things up a bit.

To bed then.

Here, I need to backtrack a bit for the benefit of those familiar only with the Venice Simplon-Orient-Express or the fancier carriages of the Trans-Siberian Railway. Perhaps you're lucky enough to have experienced them at first-hand, or at least seen them on TV travel programmes, and marvelled at the hand-stitched bed-linen, the crushed velvet drapes, the complimentary slippers and the attentive service by butlers, at whom you only need raise an eyebrow when you'd like another nightcap. In travel, as in life, you get what you pay for, and those famous and very agreeable overnight journeys – on trains pulled by unicorns, passengers soothed by whale song and tucked in at night by elves – cost thousands.

At the other end of the scale, the budget version is sitting up all night in a high-backed train seat with the lights on and the conductor poking you every now and again to have another look at your ticket. At three am the train sits in a siding for an hour or

139

so and you finally manage to fall into a fitful sleep only to be poked awake by a different kind of guard who wants to see your passport. At five am the passenger next to you starts chugging beers and clambering over your knees to go to the toilet. Don't go to the toilet yourself by the way – it's a distressing sight that will stay with you until the day you die. Use a plastic water bottle, like the guy on the other side of you.

You only travel overnight by train this way when you're young or broke. You do it because you have no choice, and you don't do it very often because what the InterRail website makes sound like a complete hoot – "Get ready to sleep your way to Berlin!" – is in fact truly and deeply uncomfortable. If you examine any of the medieval illustrations of Dante's *Inferno*, right there in the Circles of Hell, somewhere between Wrath and Violence, you'll be able to pick out the tiny, tortured figures of contorted backpackers trying to get some shut-eye on the Paris-to-Venice sleeper.

When you get a bit older and little more affluent, it's revealed to you in a hand-delivered letter on embossed parchment on your thirtieth birthday that some of the train carriages magically convert into couchettes – little bunk-beds with sheets and pillows. Your world is rocked. You mean if I just give you more of this money stuff, I can lie down and stretch out overnight? Sleep might be technically possible after all?

Even on the Zagreb-Zürich service – *sans confort* it might be – there are different classes of accommodation available, with the top-of-the-range choice being a single-person sleeping cabin with its own little sink and a turn-down service. I consider its attractions and also its hefty price. I weigh the merits of the relatively cheaper two- and four-bunk options. All seem to offer a restful night's sleep as we trundle across central Europe. However, I feel that any type of couchette is better than sitting up all night and thus opt for economy on the basis on which I make many of my travelling decisions – namely, how bad can it be?

Funny you should ask.

My cabin is one of those six-seater compartments of the sort I've been travelling in for the last couple of days. The two facing rows of three seats have made up into the bottom two bunk beds. Above them, on each side, two more beds fold down from the compartment wall, so that the six-seater cabin becomes a two-sided triple-decker bunk house.

I have one of the two top bunks, access to which is up a little ladder. There's a sheet, thin blanket and pillow provided, space at the foot of the bunk for your bag and a reading light and small storage net at the other end. This is all very nice and just as it should be. What there isn't is any headroom whatsoever. If you can picture lying on your back in a closed coffin or getting stuck underground while crawling through a cave, I'd say you have a pretty good idea of the available space for moving around in the top bunk of a six-berth cabin. Raising my head more than a few inches proves impossible – so doubling up to take off my socks, say, not a chance.

I entertain myself for a while by wrestling with the sheet, eventually managing to spread it out beneath me, and lie there breathing heavily. Similar groans and sharp intakes of breath reveal that the rest of the occupants have all arrived by now too. I have three other gulag inmates at my level in the top tiers, and we form an immediate yet unspoken bond as we peer over the edge at the two people in the spacious ground-level bunks, who are gaily swinging themselves in and out of bed, taking off their shoes and socks, sitting up, checking the contents of their bags and generally behaving in a manner likely to cause murder most foul. One of them disappears into the corridor, heads down to the train toilet and comes back shortly dressed in sleepwear, teeth presumably brushed, throat gargled and teddy bear primed for cuddling. I toy with the idea of sliding myself out horizontally, latching on to the ladder backwards, climbing down, locating the toilet, changing a T-shirt at least, returning up the ladder backwards, finding somewhere to put my discarded clothes and sliding myself back in horizontally, but it's exhausting just thinking about it. I do manage to kick my shoes off.

There. Bed-time.

I lie there, firstly on my back but it's just too weird with the ceiling so close to my eyes. I wriggle and shift, and eventually end up in a sort of lateral splay as the train rocks gently from side to side. The compartment door is slightly open and there's a shaft of natural light from the corridor which waxes and wanes as the train rattles on into the night. Slow corners tilt me one way and another, while clanks and squeals – and almost imperceptible speed changes – signal arrival at and departure from unknown stations in Slovenia and then Austria. Voices rise and fall as people walk past our cabin; below me are coughs, snuffles and snores.

In this cramped coffin-cave, sweating on a bare sheet on a humid night in central Europe, something miraculous happens. The train picks me up and carries me off, and I drift into a sleep that has a womb-like rhythm at its heart – a pulsing, rocking, breathing state that takes eight hundred kilometres and fifteen hours and condenses them into an instant or an eternity, it's hard to tell which. Train-sleep is unlike any other. I've succumbed to it before, in France, Italy, Malaysia and China – the same narrow bunks, the same sounds, the same motions leading to an ocean-like wave of acceptance as you give yourself to the rolling rails. Minutes go by in hours, and then hours in minutes, as I'm rocked in and out of consciousness by a giant metal cradle on wheels.

It's hard to believe but I have to be woken up – a touch of my shoulder by the guard who inspected my ticket the night before. It's around seven am and my stop is coming up in around an hour. I'm treated – why Ambassador, you spoil me – to a cup of instant black coffee and a cellophane-wrapped croissant, which is by no means the worst thing I have had for breakfast on a train. That would be the meal served on the overnight sleeper to Guangzhou in southeast China, where breakfast was two fried eggs and a slice of toast. Cooked the night before, wrapped in clingfilm on a plastic plate and left by the bunk at six am. As with so many things, it's the thought that counts.

143

Just after eight in the morning I'm turfed off the train at the Swiss town of Sargans. The comma-shaped Principality and micro-state of Liechtenstein is at hand.

The fourth smallest country in Europe (only Vatican City, Monaco and San Marino are smaller), sixth in the world (hello Nauru and Tuvalu), and on my list because it's a why-wouldn't-I? I could chug straight past to Zürich, just an hour away, but then I would be passing up the chance to visit – get this, geography fans – one of the world's only two double-landlocked countries. That's a landlocked country surrounded entirely by other landlocked countries – Liechtenstein being bordered by Switzerland and Austria. Uzbekistan is the other, by the way, which rather more impressively is surrounded by five other landlocked nations – basically all the Stans, huddled together with an aversion to water.

So that's why I'm delivering myself to Liechtenstein but getting there by train is a different matter, because the fourth smallest country in Europe doesn't have an international rail service. You can see their point. It's only twenty-four kilometres long from north to south and there are some chunky mountains in the middle. But if you get off at Sargans in Switzerland, there are buses that whisk you straight from the station and across the imperceptible border to the main town square in Vaduz, the capital.

It's a pretty half-hour ride made more enjoyable because, for the first time in days, the temperature isn't yet galloping towards thirty-silly degrees. I dump the backpack in a station locker and flex my shoulders in the fresh morning air. That's unusual, what is that? Actual unheated oxygen? I've almost forgotten what it's like not to breathe soup.

The bus creeps out of run-of-the-mill Sargans but we're soon in green, open countryside, barrelling along a valley bottom and then taking a convoluted route around a perfectly shaped castle on top of sculpted terraces. Forests cling to encircling mountains shrouded in low cloud and it's impossible to tell where Switzerland stops and Liechtenstein starts. Indeed, accidents of imperial history aside, as princes carved out statelets for themselves, Liechtenstein might just as easily be an alpine corner of Switzerland or Austria. It takes a keener eye than mine to discern any difference between the scenery and buildings.

Vaduz, however, is a surprise. The capital of a nation of around forty thousand people is a small town of six thousand, and while I've been expecting a chocolate-box scene of flower-fronted Heidi houses and rosy-cheeked milkmaids, the bus pulls up in front of a concrete municipal centre transported directly from 1970s inner-city Britain. It's not what you'd call scenic and doesn't improve much on the short walk to the main square, which is surrounded by low-rise resort-style apartment buildings under a sheer rock bluff. There's a World of Watches, a couple of banks and a painted Town Hall that's a bit more interesting, and that's about your lot.

Maybe I shouldn't be surprised at this lack of character. Liechtenstein boasts of having more registered companies than citizens. It's a wealthy financial centre with one of the highest standards of living in the world. Other facts and highlights to do with the country are all very definitely on the tax and economy side of the ledger (apart from the double-landlocked thing, which – fair play to them – is very cool). It's also got no airport, no army, a prison with hardly any inmates, one TV channel and a stamp museum. In short, there's not a lot going on that isn't to do with making money or saving money and I think we're beginning to get to the bottom of why downtown Vaduz resembles a civic centre designed by an accountant.

However, Liechtenstein does still have a prince as the head of state and he lives in the castle at the top of the hill above town. I'd love to believe – as Wikipedia claims – that on the country's national holiday (15 August) everyone is invited to the castle "where speeches are made and complimentary beer is served" but that seems too good to be true. "Sloshed in the Schloss" is how I would market that by the way – you're welcome Liechtenstein Tourist Board. Anyway, I'm a month early and don't think that knocking on the door for Prince Hans-Adam II von und zu Liechtenstein ("Hans-baby, I'm here for the beer!") is going to get me far. But I do climb up the steps through the woods to the castle grounds and look at the views through a telescope. Vaduz sits directly below – it really is a very small and non-descript town, set in a wide valley between green slopes.

Back down in town I follow the pedestrianised main street to the Tourist Centre where they have an extremely lucrative gig going, selling passport stamps for three euros. Time was, you got a stamp at every border in Europe, which was a nice memento of your trip. But there's no border to cross here and Liechtenstein has figured out that we are all going to be happy to part with a few euros just to prove we've been to the smallest double-landlocked country in the world ruled by a beer-drinking prince.

I pay up and sit in the square for a bit with a hilariously expensive cup of tea, and think, now what? Because my plan had been to spend most of the day here – enjoying the marvels and attractions of the principality – and jump on a late-afternoon train. But at eleven o'clock in the morning I rather feel that Vaduz and I are heading for an amicable divorce. We gave it our best shot, but it just hasn't worked out. No hard feelings and all that, but it's time for both of us to move on. In my case, from one world-renowned financial centre to another – Zürich – which might be considered a case of no-fool-like-an-old fool, given the irreconcilable differences that Vaduz and I have. What's that definition of insanity? Doing the same thing over and over again but expecting different results. Well, count me in, I'm a hopeless romantic, this time I know it will be different.

A couple of hours later I'm gliding into Zürich Hauptbahnhof, ready to be swooped off my feet. A confession – I have been here before, a youthful dalliance if you will, on my InterRail trip as a teenager, but I don't remember the city at all. More to the point, it clearly doesn't remember me. I should have thought that blowing up bits of a Swiss mountain, hacking out a footpath or two and launching a hot-air balloon would merit at least a statue. Ungallant, Zürich, that's what you are.

There's little to jog my memory around the station – huge concourse, roaring traffic, high buildings – but the minute I hit the river, the Limmat, which flows through the city from the lake at its head, the views open up and it quickly becomes apparent that Zürich is a stunner. I'm not quite prepared to go the full Leslie Phillips – in Sixties films, as the British actor first clapped eyes on a woman he would invariably describe as a "filly", the pencil-moustachioed lothario would leer and issue his signature drawl of "Ding-dong!". But Zürich certainly has something – not for nothing does it regularly figure on lists of the world's most liveable cities.

It's not the capital of Switzerland of course, Bern is, but Zürich is the largest city and has been a significant settlement since Roman times, when it was known as Turicum. Later it became a wealthy trading city and theological centre, its presiding families and nobility throwing their weight around until the establishment of the Swiss federal state in the mid-nineteenth century. There's history and heritage here, and an enduring notion that Zürich is a class act.

The location helps. The city is immediately well-formed and debonair, with grand buildings set down both sides of the wide river which flows out of Lake Zürich. The Alps are just thirty kilometres away, framing views from the lakeshore where unaffordable boats bob on glistening waters. Parks and forests wrap around the lake, while in town trams trundle, steeples soar and church bells sound. Medieval guild-houses, a stately town hall and a twelfth-century cathedral add sturdy character, while solid stone bridges carry you into the old-town areas on either side of the river. There are delightful café-bars overlooking the water and inviting restaurants of all cuisines in shady squares. All this adds up to something quite lovely and unexpected – a cultured and cultural city with much to admire.

So admire it I do, on a long stroll down the river and out to the quayside and jetties at the edge of the lake. There is a pristineness, a just-so-ness about the place, that ordinarily would grate with me (and yes, that's definitely lazy stereotyping on my part). Everything works. Everything is tidy. The river sparkles on this most sparkling of summer days. *Alles ist in ordnung.* Usually, I prefer a Mediterranean shambles (really going for the stereotypes here), a city that's a bit scruffy around the edges, but I am definitely taking a shine to Zürich.

Returning up the other side of the Limmat, I walk past a vintage wooden building with a low deck that drops right on the river. It's a *badi* – a public swimming area, this one for women only, and one of dozens set up on the Limmat and around the lake for Zürichers to cool off in summer. That's how clean the water is in city-centre Zürich – the authorities encourage you to swim in the river – which fact puts some flesh on the whole "world's most liveable city" thing. Further north from here, up beyond the station, the cool kids apparently use the river current to float down from Unterer Letten, the oldest riverside bath in the city, and then clamber out and walk back to the start for another go.

I can sense you all searching for your house deeds, looking up estate agents' details and thinking about relocating. I know, it's all very seductive. But there is something you should know which is that Zürich – indeed Switzerland – is not a cheap date. You turn up on the doorstep and Zürich's dad is going to frown at your beat-up, ten-year-old Ford Focus, enquire about your intentions and prospects and explain that Zürich is accustomed to a certain lifestyle – while indicating, with perhaps just the dip of a well-groomed eyebrow, that you are not the person he had in mind for his city. Zürich is not simply expensive, it's ruinously, astronomically, oligarchically expensive, and while I knew that before I arrived, I only knew it in a vague, general sense and thought that somehow everything would be all right; that I'd be able to wing it ("Oh the Focus? No, I'm getting a new car quite soon. And a new job. And a raise. No later than ten pm, yes sir.")

But the more I browse in shop windows along Bahnhofstrasse (Gucci, Louis Vuitton, Chanel, Cartier, Tiffany), the more my Zürich dream dies. The simplest way I can explain the order of magnitude of Swiss pricing is to pick a menu, any menu, in one of the agreeable-looking restaurants in a tree-shaded square off the river. The sort of place that, if it was in Spain, you'd barely look at the prices before ordering dinner on the understanding that food can only cost so much. It comes from the market, the chef does his magic in the kitchen and adds on a percentage, there's a bit more for the waiter and the lighting and heating, and there's your finished dish for ten or fifteen euros. As far as I understand it, in Switzerland the general policy seems to be –

start with that actual price of a dish, for a steak say, or a plate of spaghetti, double or even treble it, and then add another ten or twenty euros for a laugh. Confirm to the customer with a straight face that that is indeed what it costs, add on another five euros for a glass of water, five more for the bread-basket, and don't forget the ten-percent service charge. In posher places they do all that and then double it again, just for the hell of it.

But you know what? Life, being too short and all that? The leafy, cobbled square by the river outside the grand old Hotel Storchen really does look inviting, and the views are sparkling. Waiters in black braces and bow ties glide around with glistening trays lined with starched white linen. Cocktails are being drunk – with little umbrella sticks – and dainty snacks delivered to prosperous customers who don't look like they spent last night in a mobile metal coffin. I sit down to the single most expensive cup of coffee I have ever ordered – need to know basis I'm afraid, my accountant is probably reading this – and sip the bejeesus out of that bad boy until, about an hour later, it can be sipped no more. While I'm here I look up the room prices for a laugh – five hundred a night, and I was going to specify euros but when it's five hundred it hardly matters which currency.

I think, on the whole, I prefer a country where coffee, wine and good food are daily essentials – part of the whirl of life – and not things that cause actual, physical pain when you come to pay for them. Of course, this is mostly my fault for not being successful enough – Zürich's a ten, I'm punching seven at best, and I need to let the city go gracefully. However, if you do ever come into a windfall, a bequest from a long-lost aunt say, then I thoroughly recommend a drink at the Hotel Storchen, where you can ponder foolish ambition and unattainable beauty until they chuck you out for lingering too long over an espresso.

The Bernina Express

Switzerland would be a mighty big place if it were ironed flat. Mark Twain.

THE GREATEST TRAIN ride in Europe starts under the cavernous vaults of Zürich's main railway station, where the 7.07am to Chur is about to depart. I grab a breakfast sandwich and a coffee from one of the snack stalls − and remember to breathe deeply when they say, "And that will be twenty euros, how would you like to pay?" (The correct answer is "With a deep pain in my heart and wallet, thank you." Not "I said ONE coffee and ONE sandwich, oh right, jeez.")

Still, all will be well because I'm on my way to ride the Bernina Express, the prince of all European rail journeys − the one all the rail buffs say you should take at least once in your life. Other routes have more cachet and fame but are thunderingly pricey − think the luxury Glacier Express or the Venice Simplon-Orient-Express, either of which will set you back hundreds of euros. At the budget end of the scale, the route from Bar in Montenegro to Belgrade in Serbia is a candidate, super cheap and seriously scenic but encompassing twelve hours of back-to-basics travel in rattling, frill-free carriages. Scotland's West Highland Line? Possibly a contender, but too close to home for me to be a true adventure.

Instead, I've bided my time to travel on the Bernina Express on the understanding that there is, quite simply, nothing like it – a train ride across the largely impenetrable, glacier-scarred, lake-strewn Alps between Switzerland and Italy. It's the final leg of my trip – heading for my ninth country on my ninth day – and there's a definite feeling of having saved the best until last. I've encountered plenty of fine scenery so far, but nothing I suspect to match what's to come today as I roll due south to journey's end in Milan. The "armchair mountaineer' is what one travel guide calls the Bernina Express, so I'm expecting great – if precipitously alarming – things from the route. Given its billing as one of Europe's most dramatic rail experiences, the Bernina Express ticket is also surprisingly cheap – from thirty euros or so if booked in advance, so about the price of a Swiss cup of coffee (I just about jest).

The route itself starts in Chur, an hour or so up the line from Zürich, and because Switzerland doesn't really do un-scenic even the warm-up act is a beauty. We slide out through the suburbs and the train is soon hugging the shore of the Zürichsee, the long, thin, finger-lake that points south of the city. There's shimmering water right outside the train window and flat, green clearings on the other side of the lake where small villages hunker down under soaring peaks. After a further quick jaunt along the shore of the neighbouring Walensee, the train turns south and climbs to Chur, already a fair few hundred metres up in the Alps but only marking the start of today's cross-mountain journey.

On another day, I'd make time for Chur – it claims to be Switzerland's oldest town, though squabbles about this rage in neighbouring regions so probably best to not get involved. Chur does, however, have a very attractive, traffic-free old town with, according to the local tourist board, "an almost Mediterranean charm." Let's see. It's six hundred metres up in the Alps, with slender Germanic spires and steeply pitched roofs to cope with the snow. They've never been to the Mediterranean, have they?

Onwards though, because I have to cross platforms at Chur and change trains for the shiny red Bernina Express, which is waiting patiently at the station. From here to the Italian border town of Tirano (where I'll change again, for Milan), it's a hundred and forty-four kilometres along a route declared a World Heritage Site – or, to put it another way, four-and-a-half hours of relentlessly majestic big-sky scenery and quite extraordinary engineering. Extraordinary for any age – more so when you consider that the railway first opened in 1908, built with pick and shovel, the rocks and rubble cleared by dynamite and donkey.

Don't be fooled by the word "express," by the way. This is no high-speed rollercoaster ride through the Alps; rather a gentle trundle that forms a lifeline for mountain communities even today. Local trains ply the route daily, and while flashier panoramic and open-air carriages are added to some services for tourists, I've opted to save money by sitting in the cheaper second-class seats of one of the regular carriages. There are no advance seat reservations available for these carriages, and I don't mind telling you that this has been causing me some consternation on the way up to Chur. I've been assured that the views are the same – you're on the same Bernina Express train after all, just in a carriage a bit further down. But there seems to be general agreement that getting a seat on the righthand side is paramount, if you want the best views. And there are a lot of people on my Zürich to Chur service, all now busy positioning themselves at the doors with strategic pointy elbows as the train pulls into the station.

I fuss with the backpack and ready myself for the fray, but I needn't have worried. Most of the passengers make a beeline for the reserved panoramic carriages and I'm left to clamber leisurely aboard further down, where the count is two well-dressed vintage ladies, one middle-aged businessman with briefcase and me. There are big, clear windows and plenty of seats to spare. I choose one on the righthand side with a little fold-out table and a map of the route. And at 8.32am on the dot, we're off.

Out we go at first through suburban Chur, following one side of a gushing but otherwise unremarkable river. This is the River Rhine of all things – Europe's second longest after the Danube – which has its source a little way higher up in the Swiss Alps, rushes through Chur and then barrels another thousand kilometres north through Germany and the Netherlands to the North Sea. Soon we turn south, with the train's initial climb through alpine forests and meadows, past small towns and villages with wood-clad houses, large slatted barns and imposing church spires. Unconcerned cows graze close to the line at times, while traffic is held at barriers as the Bernina Express trundles across snaking mountain roads.

Bridges and tunnels come thick and fast, and I stop counting after a while (there are a hundred and ninety-six and fifty-five, for the record). There's hidden engineering at every point, from the pillared galleries over the tracks that act as avalanche breaks – it's high summer, relax – to the deceptive tunnels that actually curve and circle within the mountain rock. As for viaducts across deep canyons, we're broken in gently so that by the time the Landwasser viaduct comes along we're entirely relaxed about the fact that it's not only sixty-five metres high and curved – curved! how did they do that? – but that it also disappears into a snaking tunnel at the far end as if it's the world's best fairground ride. Just think about that sixty-five-metre-high viaduct for a minute – built at the turn of the twentieth century using only two cranes and without scaffolding of any kind.

Why, you might well ask? By definition – at the top of the Alps – this is a crazy place to build a railway. But with a fancy spa and ski resort at nearby St Moritz, there was always an incentive to try and drive a track over the Bernina Pass from Tirano to open up direct access for tourists. Along with the connecting Albula Railway, completed a few years earlier, the Bernina offered year-round transportation to settlements in one of the most inaccessible of mountain regions. It still carries freight – fuel, timber, building supplies – between Italy and Switzerland.

A couple of hours into the journey, the train levels out at the top of the Bernina Pass, where we're not just in the Alps – we're *on* the Alps. Glacial lakes glide by, with the train carriages reflected in the deep, clear waters. Lago Bianco marks a watershed – south of here, water flows into the Adriatic, while east it pours, runs and trickles an unfathomable distance to the Black Sea. There's snow on the nearby slopes, while hardy-looking cattle graze amongst a rock-strewn carpet of alpine wildflowers. At one point, as the train makes a mighty curve around the almost turquoise water of the lake, I can see the half-dozen panoramic carriages swinging into line behind me, a vibrant red against the green slopes.

Then suddenly there's a halt, right by the side of the water, at the highest point on the whole line – Ospizio Bernina (2,253 metres – 7,391 feet). This stop makes it the highest public railway with year-round service in the Alps, and you can hear the definition creaking in that caveat-filled sentence, since there are higher mountain railways and funiculars. But I'll happily take the accolade, as apparently does the businessman-plus-briefcase, because it's here, bafflingly, that he chooses to get off the train. I'm looking out of the window, across the lake to a sheer mountainside with snow patches, wondering quite where his office is. It's only as the train pulls off again that I turn around and look through the window on the other side of the carriage and see a very pleasant-looking rustic stone restaurant. Nice place for a meeting, and I guess if you planned it right you could get out for lunch and catch a later train. I make a note for next time.

There's another stop a little further on at the tiny halt of Alp Grüm, and this time we're given ten minutes for a quick stretch of the legs and a view of the Palü Glacier beyond, hanging in a vast alpine bowl. Apart from the quick switch at Chur, I haven't left air-conditioned comfort since seven am this morning and I step out into a bright and sunny, but not sweltering, day. These are high mountains we're in now – the Palü summit tops out at three thousand nine hundred metres – and for the first time in over a week the temperature isn't making violent assaults on my tender English person.

While everyone is busy taking glacier selfies I take the opportunity to climb into the neighbouring first-class carriage for a sneaky look. To be honest, the seats don't look any more comfortable, but not only do these passengers have the side views, they also enjoy the considerable bonus of being able to look straight out through the driver's cabin window ahead of them. Although I doubt it's that reassuring to watch the driver cover his eyes, and cross himself and his fingers, every time the train tackles another towering viaduct.

After the high mountain air of Alp Grüm, I'm thinking that the best bits of the Bernina route are behind me, but I have to say that the scenery doesn't let up on the descent into the Val Poschiavo. It's gentler perhaps, as orchards and vineyards begin to appear on both sides of the valley, and there's another lakeside panorama as we sweep past Lago di Poschiavo. Notice the names by the way. We're still in Switzerland – just – but are now travelling through the Italian-speaking part as we nudge ever close to Tirano. In a nod to the more temperate climes on this side of the Alps, the train website promises me glaciers and palm trees on the same trip, and while they've been as good as their word about the glacier there's no sign yet of any palms. However, there is something approaching that is far more sensational than a Swiss palm tree.

If the question is "How do you control a train's speed on a ridiculously steep ascent/descent of a narrow valley?", the answer is "Build a massive three-hundred-and-sixty-degree curved track – oh, and make it a viaduct." (By this time, I am beginning to understand that the solution to any engineering problem on the route was "Build a viaduct.") This is the Bernina line's last burst of hat-in-the-air exuberance, its final piece of deft design – namely the remarkable Brusio Spiral Viaduct. It's like a thin horizontal slice out of the Colosseum, set in orchard-filled fields beneath tumbling valley screes. The front of the train pretty much catches up with the back as it circles the viaduct, making for one of those photographs that looks like you have Photoshop to thank rather than a band of nameless navvies who constructed one of Europe's most spectacular structures. I am actually chortling as we round the full circle, approaching over the top of the viaduct, and then down and around to exit through the arches. Hat-tip guys, really; that's just sensational.

With superlatives long since exhausted, it only remains to trundle into Tirano – though there is a final surprise when I

160

glance out of the window and discover that the train is actually running down the main street, with houses and shops on either side. I know, no viaduct, what are they thinking? Instead, they've basically re-engineered the railway as a tram line for the last section, so you race cars through the centre of town, turn left at the junction and come to a stop at Tirano station.

I would like to take a moment to reflect. That's one of the best journeys I've ever made, anywhere in the world. I doubt that anything I write can do it full justice. I urge you to do the trip yourself and experience it first-hand. At the very least, at this point, the Bernina Express deserves the salute of a cold beer in a cobbled square, both of which Tirano seems to be able to offer me.

There is, of course, a problem, and it's do with the fact that Tirano is not in Switzerland, where everything has worked perfectly for the last four-and-a-half hours. It is in Italy.

Now I yield to no one in my love for that country and its very singular ways, but you have to be in the mood, for nothing is ever straightforward. Take the station for example. Tirano has two, right next to each other. One where you arrive on the Bernina Express, and an adjacent one where you catch the onward train to Milan – a train that I am not inclined to miss because it's hours till the next one and I really want to get to Milan and have a cold shower, a beer and a pizza.

Let's not even get started about why they have two stations. Anywhere else it would be something to do with different rail gauges or sprocket ratios. Here, in Italy, it's entirely possible that the Swiss engineer unwittingly insulted someone's mother; or that they tried to build the station on a Tuesday when any Italian knows that station-building is a job only carried out on a Wednesday. Who knows, is all I'm saying. There will be a reason, but it won't be one that would pass muster in a regular country.

There are about fifteen minutes between the trains, which – again – in any other country in the world is plenty of time to walk out of one station and walk into another a hundred metres away, buy a ticket and make your way to the platform. Once more, I refer you to the fact that Tirano is in Italy, where the following conversation occurs:

"A ticket to Milan please."

"You cannot buy a ticket to Milan at this window." [points to adjacent window which now has queue of people]

[Ten minutes later] "Hello again. A ticket to Milan please."

"Here is your ticket, the train is on Platform One. You must validate the ticket first."

"Great, where do I do that?"

"There is a machine right here on Platform One." [vague wave of hand]

"Thank …"

"But the machine on Platform One doesn't work. You must go to Platform Two, over there [another vague wave of hand]. That machine may work."

"*May* work?"

"Yes, quick, hurry, your train is leaving."

"Can't you just validate it here for me? In that machine next to you."

"No, quick. Platform Two. Or perhaps Three. Hurry."

All entirely normal of course for Italy, just thought I'd point it out. And in case you think you've spotted a loophole – you'll just buy your ticket in advance, cut out all the nonsense – it will come as little surprise to learn that while you can book advance tickets online for almost any rail journey you like in Italy, you can't buy one for the Tirano to Milan service. Naturally.

After a hair-raising cross-platform sprint against the clock, I settle in for a very rickety ride along the flat valley of the River Adda before the train turns south to run along the shore of Lake Como. There isn't, of course, any sign of a ticket inspector during the whole two-hour trip to Milan, making the whole ticket-validation business at Tirano entirely unnecessary. They just do it because they can; I think it keeps them entertained.

If you haven't arrived in Milan by train before – I have, so I know what to expect – then prepare to be impressed by Milano Centrale, Milan Central Station. One of the world's greatest railway stations – a peer of New York's Grand Central or London's St Pancras – it was built during the 1920s as a symbol of national pride and enterprise under Benito Mussolini. It's colossal and vainglorious, which goes without saying when you've got a Fascist in charge. Mussolini was never going to say, "Just make it small and discreet, don't worry if the ones in England and America are better."

163

But unlike a lot of the shallow, faux-Imperial public buildings of Fascist Italy, when Milano Centrale finally opened in 1931 it quickly attracted admirers for its monumental harmony. The vast steel and glass arches over the platforms are stunning, while the public concourses display acres of shining marble, statuary, carved pediments, mosaic tiles, stone friezes and cathedral-like embellished doorways. As is the way of the world, they've done their best to ruin any sense of grandeur by plonking in shopping galleries, café franchises and fast-food outlets "To enhance your travelling experience." Yet the space prevails in these echoing, majestic halls and all you need do is look up and around you to appreciate their sheer glorious scale. By the way, if you think the station is grand inside, wait until you stumble out into the blinding summer light on to Piazza Duca d'Aosta and turn back to look at the façade. It's a towering statement of intent – many parliament buildings and national museums can't hold a candle to Milan's main station.

A quick Metro ride later and I'm holed up in a stifling room in a three-star hotel where the only instruction issued to the interior decorator appears to have been "Brown." Material? Doesn't matter. Floorboards, bedspread, tiles, paintwork, shower curtain, bedside table, toilet and sink, even the phone – all a variation on the theme of brown, and who knew there were so many shades?

If you travel around Italy on a budget for any length of time, it's the type of small hotel you soon become familiar with. One guy on the desk downstairs in front of pigeonholes full of comedy room keys with oversized fobs, which are requisitioned if you try to leave the premises. A clattery marble staircase to a dark corridor with a faded central carpet runner. A vase of flowers that turn out on inspection to be plastic. Room door locks that wouldn't survive first contact with a decent kick. Musty bathrooms with dark mould in the corners. Heavy duty window shutters that you have to heave up and down with a cord that disappears into the wall. And one electrical socket (and one only) so fiendishly inaccessible – under the bed? behind the radiator? in the wardrobe? – that there's no prospect of using any piece of tech while it's charging.

However, Desk Guy downstairs does have a little bar – rather, a cubbyhole with a small fridge and a few bottle-laden shelves – which he tempts me with as I'm on my way out to dinner. He also wants to chat, and we start in Italian because I always rather think of myself as a speaker of Italian until, usually, the second question.

The first question, in English, goes something like "Where are you from?"

I reply, in Italian, "I'm English, I love Italy. I can speak a little Italian."

And the second question, now in Italian, then proceeds at great length, pace and volume, allowing for neither pause of breath nor comprehension at any level because, in truth, all I can do is read a menu, ask where the train station is and say things like *Sono Inglese, Io amo l'Italia, Io posso parlare un po d'Italiano* (I'm

165

English, I love Italy. I can speak a little Italian). None of which is really the basis for any kind of in-depth conversation.

After we've agreed that it will be better if we speak English, Desk Guy pours me a cold beer and shares his views on the desirability of Milan as a place to live. He's a big fan. Moved here from somewhere else in the north of Italy forty years ago and would never live anywhere else. The public transport system is excellent. The city is very clean and things work. It's a good place for business, no problems. If you want a job, you can find one. It's safe, not too much crime. All in all, Milan is a great place to live, much better than …

I know exactly what's coming. I've heard it many times. He's going to say …

The South.

It's a moveable line for many in northern Italy. For some, they count anything lower than Rome; for others the South starts in Naples; and they all definitely mean the wild extremities of Calabria and Sicily. The South. The other Italy. The basket-case pieces of the country that the North pays for. In fact, Desk Guy doesn't even need to say it because he's already flagged up all the things that he thinks are wrong with the South by highlighting the marvels of Milan. There's a big chunk of his own country that can be casually dismissed as crime ridden, mafia-bedevilled, lazy, dirty and broken – even to a tourist whose mind he cannot know.

He – and others like him – have a single scintilla of a sliver of a cultural point. Milan is very different from the cities of the South. It looks north to central Europe; it's closer to Switzerland

and the Alps than it is to its own capital. It's a financial centre with a long and prosperous independent history. It feels European and not Mediterranean in the most general of senses. That should be enough to be proud of, I would venture. It's an odd sort of pride that boosts your city by disparaging half of the country, and there's an ugly undercurrent in any case. Unsaid so far by Desk Guy, but absolutely said by others – that of course they're "Arabs" and "Africans" in the South, so what can you expect?

(Possibly Racist) Desk Guy doesn't know that I've lived in Sicily and written a book about it, that I love the place like no other in Europe. It's a true melting-pot of cultures, an island unlike any other, where Phoenician, Greek, Roman, Arab, Norman, Spanish and North African influences have permeated the food, festivals, language, art and architecture. It's part of Italy but it's barely Italian in any sense that many northerners will accept. I just don't happen to think that's a bad thing. There's room for both sorts of Italy in Italy. I like Milan but I prefer it in Sicily, and that doesn't make one place better than the other. I could tell Desk Guy this and he'd doubtless talk approvingly of the things he doesn't find threatening about the South – the Greek temples, the beaches and Roman amphitheatres – but he's already shown his colours and I can't be bothered. I thank him for the beer, pay up, hand over the ridiculously over-fobbed key and stride off in search of a pizza. (Pizza, by the way mate – almost certainly Persian, Greek or Etruscan in origin, not from

Milan, so think on. Bloody Etruscans, coming over here, bringing their delicious oven-baked, bread-based snacks.)

As it is the end of the trip, following a largely fabulous day, I deserve to be eating the best pizza in Milan, which current opinion has it is at Pizza AM, not far from Porta Romana. I get there just before opening time with the shutters still down, and there's already a queue, but no matter because the affable owner walks the line dispensing free pizza squares and a glass of *Prosecco* to anyone waiting for a table. The cramped interior looks like Mirò got to decorate a Mexican *cantina*, which is kind of fun – it's all splashes and stars and primary colours – and I'm eventually given a table and a menu.

In Italy, choosing a pizza is generally fairly simple. You get your basic *margherita* with cheese and tomato and then a handful of other choices with straightforward toppings. There's no truck with sweetcorn or pineapple or any of the other abominations visited upon pizzas by foreigners, and even new-wave artisan places tend to be all about the quality and provenance of the cheese, tomatoes, flour and oil rather than adding tandoori chicken or chilli con carne to the pizzas. Possibly Italy's most famous old-school pizzeria, Da Michele in Naples – the one in *Eat, Pray, Love* that's generally considered to be among the best there is – only serves two types of pizza. You can have a *marinara* (tomatoes, oil, oregano and garlic) or a *margherita* and that's your lot. People queue for hours to get in here. No one would even think of asking them to shove some extra ham and tuna on one of those pizzas; there would certainly be some lusty Neapolitan shouting if you did.

Pizza AM sides with tradition, though with hipster add-ons. There's a short menu of around half a dozen pizzas, all of which are variations of a *margherita* except one that includes anchovies. The ingredients are lovingly detailed – *pomodorini* (cherry tomatoes) from Sicily, Calabrian wild oregano, Tuscan extra-virgin olive oil, smoked Provola cheese – and for nine to ten euros a pop they are an absolute bargain. Mine appears quick-smart out of the wood-burning oven, blackened and pockmarked with charcoal in all the right places. I slice and then tear and eat with my hands – true Italian style – and, while I'm at it, wade my way through a couple of glasses of an astoundingly drinkable local Nebbiolo red. I look it up later. Wine writer Jancis Robinson says she can taste "Roses, autumn undergrowth, woodsmoke, violets and tar." Me, I can taste life being very, very good.

When it comes, the bill already includes the mysterious Italian *coperto* or cover charge – a couple of euros per person, charged for no apparent rhyme or reason. That will do many Italians – you don't have to leave a big tip, maybe just round up a couple of euros – but being frighteningly English and not wanting to get into any trouble I leave ten percent in the dish on the way out. The owner smiles, bangs a little brass gong and everyone in the restaurant cheers, which in my opinion is exactly the way every day should end.

Milan

Many times the wrong train took me to the right place. Paulo Coelho.

MILAN IS THE end of the line. I've got one last train to catch, an afternoon service out to the airport from Milan Centrale. Until then my time is my own. And now it's almost over, on my last day, here's a question. As I've ridden the rails and seen the sights on a nine-day, nine-country, nine-city European train tour, have I been at work or on holiday?

It's something that has been nagging at me throughout the trip, a matter that I haven't fully resolved. After all, the tour has featured many of the elements of a work trip, not least a relentless slog of a schedule. Then again, no one made me do it. I volunteered for this. Traipsing around random European cities one after another might not sound like your idea of a holiday, but this is the sort of thing I do for fun anyway. It's just that I don't always write a book about it afterwards.

As it happens, there's a simple way to decide the matter.

On the last day of my holiday, after an exhausting nine-day trip criss-crossing Europe by train, I take the rare chance to sleep in late. No seven am station departure for me today. I get up at about nine and head downstairs to the hotel lobby where (Possibly Racist) Desk Guy has put out croissants and coffee. That – together with a leisurely flick through the news app on my

170

phone – gets me to about ten o'clock, after which I put on my cleanest clothes and pack my rucksack for the final time. Desk Guy holds the bag for me in his little storeroom, while I ponder the rising heat outside and realise that there isn't anything I want to see that's worth getting hot and bothered about before my flight. I head down the road to the nearest café, spend another hour there in the shade sipping a *macchiato*, and then return to the hotel where Desk Guy orders me a taxi for the station. I'm still pretty early for the airport train but figure it will be pleasant to have an early lunch at the station in air-conditioned comfort, before riding out to the airport in plenty of time for my flight home. If there's time to kill I can drink more coffee, read my book and relax.

Yup, if I was on holiday, that's definitely what I would do.

Instead, I am – *checks surroundings, wipes sweating brow, peels T-shirt from skin, shakes head* – on a packed metro train riding the few stops to Consiliazione station. And I'm doing this because I don't really have holidays. Not any more.

I did. Once upon a time, I booked relaxing holidays, didn't plan too much and came back refreshed. I read some books, went on walks, ate in random restaurants, drank in the same bar every night because it was great, went to the museum but it was closed so opted for a lazy lunch instead, and didn't go on any of the day trips because it was just too hot. But then I got a job as a travel writer. I needed notes and photos to jog my memory and polish my story when I got home again. I required facts, descriptions and information. A drink in the same bar every night wasn't

171

really going to cut it if I hoped to take the true pulse of a resort; eating in the first restaurant I came across might mean I never got to taste the best of the local cuisine. I had to get to work.

Of course, it's all a question of degree. I'm fully aware that most people put "work" in inverted commas when they mention it in relation to travel-writing. You'll be doing the little curly-air-quote thing with your fingers now, I know it. It's not that I'm complaining or saying my job is particularly hard. But being at work rather than on holiday soon started to become my default setting. My travel-writing brain began to take over on even the most innocent of trips. Holiday Brain basically didn't give a stuff – too busy contemplating sunset margaritas – so Travel-Writing Brain just marched right in and took over.

Relaxing weekend away? "This will make a great story for the blog," I think, as I stroll through the local market. "I'm just going back to get a photo," I find myself saying. Or – "You go on ahead, I want to spend a bit more time here and make some notes." Listen to myself – notes! I'm supposed to be on holiday. Only there are no more holidays, because I'm now always on the look-out for the angle and the story. Even if I'm not planning on writing about this exact location or experience, I never know when it might come in handy to have some extra photos, a description of a neighbourhood and the addresses of three more local restaurants.

In fact, restaurants are the worst. I will gladly walk down as many back streets and through as many out-of-the-way neighbourhoods as possible in search of a great meal. I arrive with a long list of 'possibles' and 'maybes' and tick them off as I go, and even when I think I have found the perfect place, I can always persuade myself that there is a better restaurant just around the corner, if only I would go and see. And so off I go, and occasionally there is a better place, but often there isn't, and then I have to tramp back to the previous restaurant – now full of laughing, eating, happy people, with no tables available for hours – and settle for dinner instead someplace else that isn't really that great or atmospheric. And I can tell you from experience, if you try this sort of thing with a travel companion when you're on holiday, and not officially working, then you can expect a frosty exchange of views. This sort of thing.

Frosty Person: "We could have eaten in that really nice restaurant. Half an hour ago. Instead of here [indicating dismal nature of current establishment with sweep of hand]".

Me: "I know, but it was the first one we looked at."

Frosty Person: "So? They were all eating nice food and having a nice time [indicating truth of statement with gesture at un-nice food and un-nice time in current un-nice establishment]".

Me: [aghast] "But you can't just go into the first restaurant you come across. There might be a better one somewhere else."

Frosty Person: [fixing me with gimlet-eyed stare] "Are you mad? You're not in charge of choosing restaurants anymore. Get used to it, buster."

All of which is why I am currently rubbing sweaty shoulders with local commuters on the metro.

173

I am constitutionally unable to take it easy, even on my last day. And true to form, there is of course a restaurant that I plan to check out. But first I want to go and see something in Milan, even though it is going to require charging around like an idiot for a few hours instead of sitting quietly in a café reading a book.

I could go into the centre and gawp at the Duomo, the cathedral, but I've been before several times. It's magnificent, make no mistake – the biggest Gothic cathedral in the world and the largest church in Italy, the second fact being the one that will win you a pub quiz one day (because St Peter's in Rome, which is bigger, is actually in the Vatican City). If you haven't seen Milan's cathedral then you absolutely should – a frothy confection of stone pinnacles, elaborate tracery and intricately carved statues that anchors a vast and blindingly white square across which march troupes of flag-led tour groups. Oscar Wilde did not like it one bit – "An awful failure … monstrous and inartistic …everything is vile" – but that's Rough Guide writers for you. Snarky. While you're there, pay to go up on the roof terrace and you get one of the best views in any city, peering out over rooftops between delicate stonework crafted by master masons over several hundred years.

If not the Duomo, then maybe the adjacent Galleria Vittorio Emanuele II? It's where loaded *milanese* go to shop for baubles and eat dainty pastries and the rest of us go to stare with astonishment at the ludicrous excess and contemplate the overthrow of consumer capitalism. Think of any fancy glass-roofed shopping mall you've ever been in, and Milan's Galleria

174

says "Oh dear me, no. Bless, that's not how you do it." This is a mall amongst malls, built to truly regal specifications in the 1860s, with two crossed, glass-vaulted, arched arcades topped by a majestic glass dome. In the central octagon there are heavily trod-upon mosaics and you won't have to wait very long to see someone spin around on their heels three times for luck on the tile-depicted gonads of a very unfortunate bull. The marble gallery floors themselves are so polished and shiny that they simply demand a good long run-up and a full knee-slide by a phalanx of Extinction Rebellion protestors. Needless to say, I've never bought or eaten anything in here and today doesn't seem like the day I'm going to start sipping Campari-sodas and sizing up Louis Vuitton man-bags.

The whole centre of Milan is one big bling-fest. Showing off is what it does best. On the other side of the Galleria you emerge on the street across from the opera house – not just any old opera house but La Scala, probably the most famous one in the world. Behind here – the Quadrilatero d'Oro (Golden Rectangle) fashion district, with show-stopping window displays by internationally renowned designers. Up the road – the Pinacoteca di Brera, choc-full of Renaissance masterpieces. The churches get in on the act too. Take Santa Maria delle Grazie, a perfectly charming fifteenth-century church and convent. When the Duke of Milan had it rebuilt to serve as his family pantheon, he commissioned an acclaimed artist to paint a mural on the wall of a room that later became a refectory. Which is why the world's most famous religious painting – *The Last Supper* by Leonardo da

Vinci – is on the dining room wall of Milan's Chiesa di Santa Maria delle Grazie, just a five-minute walk from Consiliazione metro station.

We could debate whether or not it's worth booking in advance and queuing up for an expensive, timed-ticket, half-hour session spent looking at a picture of thirteen blokes at a very long table. After all, it is *The Last Supper* by Leonardo da Vinci – second only to the *Mona Lisa* in its fame. Yet again, it isn't really, not anymore, since the painting began to deteriorate almost immediately after it was finished, as Leonardo had used an inferior fresco technique. Over the next four hundred years it was variously damaged, chipped, scratched, flooded and even rattled by bombs. French troops reputedly threw stones at it; dodgy restorers coloured in bits and re-drew some of the figures; even the last great restoration, which took twenty-one years, divided the art world after attempts were made to return the fresco closer to its original form. I suspect there's not a brushstroke on there now that Leonardo would recognise as his own.

Thankfully, I don't have to get involved in any of this. I've seen it before. Go, don't go, I don't mind. (Just don't throw stones at it or colour bits in, they're fussy about that.) I've come out to Consiliazione not for *The Final Dinner* but for another stop on the da Vinci trail, which is just across the road but far less well-known. I've come to see a vineyard.

Leonardo was originally from Tuscany, joined an artist's workshop as a teenager and later moved to Milan, where he worked largely for the Duke, Ludovico Sforza. It was Sforza who commissioned *The Ultimate Snack*, which was completed in around 1498, and the Duke was so delighted with his efforts that he gave Leonardo a vineyard (a *vigna*) near what is now Corso Magenta. It lay in the middle of fields – hard to believe now – at the back of the Casa degli Atellani, a Renaissance *palazzo* belonging to more of the Duke's courtiers and hangers-on. Leonardo passed on the vineyard in his will to his servants, but after that the wine trail goes cold and the vineyard was lost to history. The Atellani *palazzo*, however, survived the centuries and thanks to a bit of sleuthing by earlier owners, the vineyard site was identified in the grounds and re-planted with vines of the type popular in fifteenth-century Milan.

All right, yes, granted, it's not Leonardo's actual vineyard then. But if they're claiming that *The Terminal Meal* over the road really is the actual *Concluding Repast*, then I think we can go with the veracity of the vineyard as well.

There are milling crowds at Santa Maria delle Grazie and hardly anybody waiting to join the next self-guided tour of La Vigna di Leonardo, so that is recommendation aplenty in my book. Access to the gardens and vineyard is through the courtyard and several rooms of the restored *palazzo*, which is a real delight in itself – there aren't many surviving Renaissance houses like this around, certainly not in Milan, and the traffic and noise of the city melts away as I glide from room to room. A colonnaded, vine-clad courtyard, frescoed ceilings, mosaic floors, a wood-panelled study – I should think it was very agreeable being the Duke's righthand man in Milan in the 1490s (at least until the Duke was overthrown in 1499 and everyone associated with him, Leonardo included, had to leg it to avoid any terminal unpleasantness).

I slowly mooch out into the formal gardens at the rear, where feral cats are occupying all the best spots in the shade. It's been laid out rather nicely, with a series of stone paths and box hedges and an avenue of trees, at the end of which is the famous vineyard. Smaller than perhaps I'm expecting, and overlooked by contemporary *milanese* housing, but a piece of history nonetheless and connected – however far removed – to one of the greatest minds that ever lived. It's said, though admittedly without much evidence, that Leonardo retired here in the evenings after working on his fresco to sip a glass or two of wine made from the same *malvasia di candia* grapes that are being grown here again today. It is lovely and quiet, with a faint rustle in the leaves from a whisper of a breeze. I can definitely see him here, with his paint-smudged fingers, taking the edge of another hard day at the old fresco painting. Let's not begrudge him his glass of wine.

Like the Hundertwasserhaus in Vienna, or underground Prague, or Bratislava's Communist-era housing estate, Leonardo's vineyard wouldn't be first on anyone's list of things to do. But – as with all those places – it stands for something in a city that's changed faces many times over the centuries. Maybe you haven't been to Milan until you've seen the Duomo, the Galleria Vittorio Emanuele and *The Last Supper*. But Milan hasn't

178

shown you all its secrets until you've also sought out Leonardo's vineyard, that's for sure. I'm glad I came.

I've got one last stop today, back across town, before finally heading out on the train to the airport. All I have is a scribbled name and address on a piece of paper from a recommendation I was given, and if you thought "city centre vineyard" was a stretch, then try "Milan farmhouse" for size.

I work my way back to the metro station and whisk the few stops around to Porta Romana, a busy area on the periphery of the old centre. Outside the metro, on one of the street junctions is the single most Italian road sign I have ever seen:

"The road ahead will be closed from August 2015 to December 2019."

Not four and a half days or weeks. Four and a half years. This is why I love Italy. No one local reads that sign and thinks there's anything wrong. Entirely normal, to close a road for four and half years and not say why.

I plod on down a nondescript street past identikit apartment blocks looking, without much hope given the surroundings, for a farmhouse, the Cascina Cuccagna. It's usually at this point that Frosty Person – remember them? – starts looking dangerously at me and muttering things like "Farmhouse? Really? What was wrong with that pizzeria?" I find in these circumstances it's best to press on, don't catch their eye, look like you know where you're going. And so I do, and there, improbably, extraordinarily, it is.

Milan didn't always sprawl, seemingly endlessly, across the plain towards the foothills of the Alps. The population never climbed much above two hundred thousand until the industrialisation of the nineteenth century, and for most of its existence it was a tightly knit – if wealthy – little northern enclave. The sort of place where dukes could bestow vineyards in the middle of the city and farms encroached upon the medieval core. The Cuccagna farm dates from the seventeenth century and stands in an otherwise unremarkable part of the modern city. Rescued after years of dereliction, today it survives as a cultural enterprise, with a restaurant, bar, deli and guest rooms, plus a few more sympathetic businesses contained within its walls.

I stroll in through the gate and it's immediately enchanting. Outside, Milan. Inside, well Milan too, but with a very endearing and laidback twist. A ring of restored buildings encircles courtyards and gardens, including vegetable and herb plots and a small orchard. Happy people are sat at benches under vines eating and drinking – there's even a farmers' market here most weeks with, I'm betting, cheery whiskered chaps in overalls selling nobbly veg from a sit-up-and-beg bicycle. I suspect that if you wanted a chat about arable crop rotation or beehive maintenance, there would be someone on hand to help out. I'm here in time for lunch – my last supper, if you like – and I can't imagine a better place to end the trip than on this shaded outdoor terrace, overlooking an unexpected slice of rustic city life.

There is a printed menu, but only for dinner, which is a shame because it sounds amazing. It's the sort of place where they know the names of the pigs that have given up their little porky lives so that you can dine on cold cuts and cured hams. There isn't a dish that doesn't namecheck a farm, a butcher or a fishmonger, while the words artisan, organic, traditional and sustainable are draped across dish descriptions with the effusive abandon of a hipster in a warehouse of vintage waistcoats. There's grilled chicken, for example. I'm not sure I need to know any more than that. Sounds delicious. The menu takes seventy-five words to describe it, I counted them.

However, that's dinner. At lunch apparently you have to run the gauntlet of the set menu, where a waiter stands in front of you and rattles off the three things you can have for a starter and the three things you can choose from for a main course. Doesn't sound hard, right? I don't know if you've ever had to do this in Italy, in Italian, but it's basically a random stab in the dark if your language skills, like mine, are more at the "Where is the bus stop" end of the spectrum. During the quickfire recitation – absolutely zero allowance made for foreigners, quite as it should be, no complaints here – there will be words you recognise, like *maiale* (pork). You grasp at it like a banker on bonus day and say gratefully, "*Sì!*", which is how I once ended up with a dish of *zamponi di maiale*, which are pigs' trotters and not at all what is required if you thought you were ordering grilled pork steaks.

I say "*Sì!*" to two dishes that, potentially, are *spaghetti aglio, olio e peperoncino* – the spaghetti isn't potential, I definitely understood that – and *fritto misto*; theoretically, I'm getting pasta with garlic, olive oil and chillies, followed by mixed fried fish. I sit back, I drink from a chilled glass of organic white wine that takes another fifty words to describe ("a persistent finish that recalls hints of Mediterranean forest with an almond aftertaste" is a mere extract) and contemplate life in all its puzzling wonder and glory.

What is it I have spent nine hectic days doing? This has barely been a travel adventure, in the Paul Theroux, Redmond O'Hanlan, Wilfrid Thesiger meaning of the word. Patagonian railways have not been ridden. Amazonian rivers have not been traced to their source. Marsh Arabs have not been befriended. It's not even been a Bill Bryson-esque continental jaunt, though I have nicked and adapted a few of his jokes. I did not cross the Andes by frog or travel around a country with a domestic appliance. I failed to encounter my heart of darkness or endure a holiday in hell. Instead I organised a train trip in Europe to some fairly familiar places and it went quite well. The track I have been on was well and truly beaten. This trip was not a stretch for me. It is the sort of thing I've been doing for years, only this time there was no paid commission, no rhyme, no reason. So, what was the point?

Have I been trying to rediscover my youth? God, I hope not. I was a horribly awkward eighteen-year-old and my teenage summer of travel – the golden InterRail period – did little to change the person I remained for many years. Timid, impressionable, scared, sarcastic, pessimistic – hello, my name was Jules. I became a writer in spite of myself – I certainly had no qualifications for it – and bumbled through the first few years, feeling like a fraud. I knew absolutely nothing about the places I wrote about, other than the things I'd managed to glean on a trip or filch from newspaper articles and books. I realise now that we all feel like this when we're young. We don't know anything, how could we? Then we find something we love. It's exciting, it's different, we wing it, it sweeps us up, until one day – a year, five, ten years later – it's just what we do. We've got away with it. Oh look, I became a travel writer.

Maybe I've been exploring whether the world is safe enough for my own children? After all, it's not long until they'll come home one day and say "Dad, I'm off to Tashkent on the train to a festival, have you got any money?" (They already say, "Have you got any money," it's the Tashkent-by-train bit that will be new). It must have been far more unnerving for my Mum to launch her boy across Europe by train in the dark ages of 1980, reliant upon me being thoughtful enough (I wasn't) to call her from a payphone now and again; at least I'll be able to text them daily, tell them the football results, warn them of coups, that sort of thing. Even so, it will require superhuman emotional restraint on my part as I stand at the station and wave goodbye to their childhood. I will definitely have something in my eye, I can tell you that. But I have checked out Europe's train system for them and seen that the apps, phones, wifi and ATMs work. It'll be fine, at least until they get to the Urals. After that, they're on their own.

Aha, here comes the starter. *Spaghetti aglio, olio e peperoncino* is one of the world's greatest and simplest dishes. Anyone can make a half-decent one. It's spaghetti tossed with good olive oil, in which you've braised some garlic and flakes of red chilli – add ground pepper, chuck in some fresh parsley, that's it. There's nothing here that can go wrong, and this is a brilliantly punchy version served in a deep, white bowl. I attack it with gusto, twirling the pasta with a Bunteresque verve, flicking oil droplets into the atmosphere and down my shirt. Up next, the fritto misto. In the worst Italian restaurants, this is a passable plate of deep-fried, lightly battered squid and prawns plundered from the freezer. In the very excellent farm restaurant, it's a retro paper cone filled with plump fried whitebait and curls of crispy fish fillets from a fishmonger they are on first-name terms with. A squeeze of lemon cuts through the wispy batter. For dipping and slurping, there's a garlicky, weapons-grade *aioli*. I look around me as I eat. Not a tourist in sight, just a bunch of happy Italians having a largely organic, sustainably sourced lunch in a farmhouse in Milan.

I think that a big chunk of the reason I took this trip is right here on this table. Not so much this lunch, as the previously unknown *possibility* of this lunch.

My long-buried InterRail pass was the catalyst, of course. Fishing it out of its shoebox took me back to the beginning. Back then, everything was new. Each handwritten railpass entry – I can see them still – was a first journey and a novel experience: Venice to Vienna, Luxembourg to Brussels, Hamburg to Copenhagen. My eyes were opened to a planet of possibilities. Every journey I made, every place I visited, added a layer to the person I slowly became; and in time the layers added up to a travel writer. An experience here, a bit of language there, some cultural knowledge, an appreciation of difference, an embrace of new things – these are the layers that the world can give you.

I realise too how lucky I am in the parents I was dealt. I got them, they got me, it all worked out very well. Long before I knew anything about – well – anything, my well-travelled, socially responsible, culturally connected folks had been busy adding their own layers to their impressionable son. Dad was an internationalist in every sense of the word. He saw people, where others see countries and borders, and he exposed our family from the outset to a life shared with other ideas and cultures. My sister got grass skirts from his trip to Fiji; the first babysitters we ever had were Dad's Cypriot students; and the first wedding meal we ever ate was an Indian banquet at a house in Huddersfield. Dad said, "Shall we drive to Lake Como in Italy for a holiday?" – in 1973 in a Renault 4, it took days – and mum said, "Sure Ken," not "With two small children? Are you mad?" The possibilities of this world were endless to my father; a life in travel was layered on from an early age, whether I knew it or not.

Layers get compacted though. Layers become hardened. And travel writers can become old – that's not their fault – and jaded – which is.

I once went on an all-expenses paid press trip to New Zealand with a very well-known writer among the other journos. The trip was an outdoor adventure involving wilderness hiking, jet-boating and jeep-driving, all of which was known in advance and sounded extremely exciting. Cut to the first day, where we were dropped off by helicopter in a bush clearing before hiking an hour or so to a shallow but icy river. Here, the guide had us remove our boots before crossing to the other side, putting them back on and continuing along the path. One of us – not me, in case you were wondering where this was going – refused. Cold water, boots off and boots on seemed like more effort than a well-known travel writer was prepared to make on an outback adventure trip. They didn't really "do" this kind of thing apparently. Not only that, they required the guide use the radio to call the helicopter back, pick them up and take them to the hotel. The rest of us stood there, aghast, watching shameless entitlement unfold on the opposite side of a narrow, inconsequential river in the New Zealand bush.

I've never wanted to be that person and Dad, while he was alive, would never have allowed it. Forty years after my first European adventure, I'm still looking for layers. I don't subscribe to the view that the world has got smaller and that everywhere is the same. You just need to look closer and harder, and make a bit more of an effort. Put the guidebook down, log out of Instagram and choose not to follow the crowds. Make up your own itinerary, whether you're exploring your own back yard or Baku. Do your own thing and new bits of the world will reveal themselves to you. Be curious. Be open to possibilities. That's what travel boils down to. Take your boots off and cross that river.

That's what I try to do, decades into my travelling life. If there are two hours between trains, I'll always use the time to stroll into whichever one-horse town it is and look around. You never know, maybe it will be my turn with the horse. If there's a celebrated rail route over impassable alps, I want to ride it. Backstreet markets with restaurants, I'm going to go and have a look. Improbable museums, slices of cake, side-trips, stopovers and tiny landlocked countries, count me in.

Wherever I've been, and however many times I've been there, I work on the basis that there's always something new to see and experience. In Vienna, that meant gigantic butterflies landing on my head and a cartoon-style building with no straight lines. In Bratislava, it was a housing estate and tales of a Socialist upbringing. Zagreb, a Sri Lankan curry and a jazz bar. Ljubljana – an old prison and an introduction to Serbian cuisine. I've been to Milan many times, but it took until this visit to find myself sitting here enjoying lunch in a seventeenth-century farmhouse in the middle of Europe's designer fashion capital. My next time in Milan? Who knows, that's the point.

I could see the traveller I would become in that old InterRail pass, but not the person. That took time. You remember what I said about the eighteen-year-old me? Timid, impressionable, scared, sarcastic, pessimistic. I worked on those and eventually I got rid of timid, impressionable and scared. The layers of travel helped with that. Things happen, plans change, your itinerary gets shot to bits. Sometimes in a foreign country, where you don't speak the language and don't know what's going on, you just have to step up. And once you've done that a few times it's easier to think, "Do you know what, I can do this."

Sarcastic, I do my best to avoid. Sorry if it creeps in every now and again. I'm not sure my sense of humour always translates straight on the page. If things make me laugh, I like to write about them, but I never plan on being mean.

But pessimistic – there's the tricky one. That sits there still, tucked in between the layers. I've been on a thousand trains – at least – but I'm still always concerned that I won't have time to make the next connection. I jump on, I wait, I look at my phone, I check the timetable, I look up at every screech of the brakes, I fear the long wait in the sidings just outside the station. Also, I look at the glorious weather and just know that it will be raining tomorrow. The hotel will be fully booked; the restaurant won't be good enough; the glass will be half-empty. And this train trip, across half a continent, on a dozen different routes, with only a night in each place and no room for error – this was a hugely complex trip to organise, and that's before you factor in that Europe has basically been melting around me in an unprecedented heatwave. I said it myself, I put it right there on the book cover, because deep down, even after all these years, I still have a default setting of pessimistic.

What could possibly go wrong? That's what I asked, in that knowing, inviting way that really means "everything."

Well here's the joy of travel. Nothing much goes wrong, most of the time. Even the things that do go awry – a missed connection, a ridiculously hot day, drunks in your carriage, a dodgy hotel room – aren't really important. They're definitely not worth worrying about in advance or getting worked up about afterwards. Dad taught me that, when we travelled together in later years to Spain and Portugal.

"I'll come along to help with the driving," he said, and two thousand miles later he still hadn't so much as sat in the driver's seat. He navigated, which involved me saying "As long as we don't have to drive through the centre of Barcelona, I'll be fine" and him saying, "OK, turn left here," which entirely predictably led to us driving right through the centre of Barcelona in rush hour.

"I knew this would happen," I said, gripping the steering wheel as Catalan drivers entertained themselves by horn-hooting, under-taking and gesticulating.

"Just keep calm," said Dad, "we get to see Barcelona too. What's the worst that can happen? Watch that articulated truck."

I'm not big on quoting former Conservative Prime Ministers, but I give you Arthur James Balfour on the subject – AJ, Big Arf – who was spot on: "Nothing matters very much and few things matter at all." The stuff that goes wrong, when you travel, is the stuff that *is* travel. They are the experiences you remember; they are the layers that accrue.

Mostly, nothing goes wrong. The pessimism is uncalled for, it always has been. My worry was that this trip would be uncool. Literally, figuratively, whatever. I thought I'd be too old to chase around Europe like a teenager; and that the heat would make it something of a gruelling challenge.

Not cool? It's been no such thing. More experiences have been had; more layers have been added.

I have one more train ride to take – out to the airport and home – and, because nothing will go wrong on the way, I have time for ice cream.

So again, here's why I love Italy in particular, and why I never tire of travel.

"Ooh, ice cream," I say to the waiter, not yet in terrible Italian, because even I know the word *gelato*.

"I'll have coconut and pistachio," I say. I like coconut and pistachio.

"No," says the waiter.

"Excuse me?"

"You can't have coconut and pistachio."

"And pray, why not? Have you run out?"

"No. Because they don't go together. You can have strawberry and mint." And with that – in his mind – unassailable argument, the waiter goes off to fetch two ice cream flavours that I don't really want.

Entirely Italian? Oh yes. But disastrous, another thing gone wrong? Not in the slightest. It makes me laugh, it's another stitch in life's rich tapestry, it's another layer.

It's cool.

From the Author

THANKS SO MUCH for reading my book – I know there's lots of choice out there and I'm just delighted that I could share some of my travels and experiences with you.

If you'd like to grab a free ebook while you're here, and travel for a bit longer in my company, then please do sign up for my Takoradi Travel Club. You'll get a free, no-obligation download of *The Travel Writer Chronicles*, containing exclusive tales and tips for aspiring travel writers.

Just head over to my website, julestoldme.com, to find out more.

Did You Like This Book?

WELL OF COURSE, I hope you did!

But as an author, there's no real way for me to tell if you enjoyed reading my book, unless you take a minute to leave a rating or a review.

Why is this important? I thought I'd take a minute myself to explain what a huge difference it makes, especially to independent authors, when kind readers leave a rating or review about a book they've read.

Firstly, I get to hear directly how much you liked the book. It's a thrill when anyone buys my work, and I get another buzz when I hear how you felt about my writing and my travel experiences. Mostly, I just sit here, writing stories and sending them out into the world. It's great when they bounce back from a reader with some feedback, whatever that might be.

The other reason is that, of course, I'd like as many people as possible to read my books. Ratings and reviews really help with publicising my books to a wider audience. In fact, after buying and reading a book, the single best thing you can do to help an author whose work you like is to leave them a review.

So, many thanks in advance, and happy travels!

Looking for Something Else to Read?

JOIN ME ON my journey in my two travel memoirs:

Don't Eat the Puffin: Tales From a Travel Writer's Life

Never Pack an Ice-Axe: Tales From a Travel Writer's Life

The exotic destinations come thick and fast – Hong Kong, Hawaii, Huddersfield – as I navigate what it means to be a travel writer in a world with endless surprises up its sleeve.

Here's an extract – from the day I spent mushing huskies in Ontario, Canada.

***

"Hold this," says our guide. "You don't have to do anything else. The dogs will just run. They follow the ones in front."

Come on, I've seen the movies. This doesn't sound right.

"So there's nothing else I need to do? Don't I shout – well, you know, 'mush' or something?"

"If you want." There's an audible snigger from the guide. "But it doesn't make any difference."

And that was Lesson One on my day out with a husky team in Ontario, Canada. It's a fantastic experience – one of life's real thrills, running with (sort of) wolves – but here's what they don't tell you about sledding with a husky team.

* * *

No one shouts mush.

I did my homework, especially for the occasion, and learned from multiple sources that you shout "mush" at huskies because it's derived from the French *marcher* (to go, to run).

Surely they shout "mush!" I'm pretty sure there's mushing in Jack London's *The Call of the Wild*; there was definitely mushing when – much against her wishes – I roped my sister to the sled when we were kids. You've got huskies, you yell mush, that's just the way it is. You'd think it would be enshrined in Canadian law to shout "mush" at a team of huskies.

But it isn't and they don't, which is obviously a huge disappointment. So just for fun you shout "mush" yourself, which is kind of entertaining until you quickly realise that there's all sorts of other stuff you really should be concentrating on. Like the fact that. . .

* * *

Huskies run really, really fast … and I mean really fast. And while it's one thing to watch a dog running fast and say "My, that pooch can move," it's entirely another to be at ground level behind several such pooches, being hauled along at the speed of light. They tell you afterwards a husky's top speed is about twenty-five mph, and I tell you there's another zero on there for sure.

So forget all about gaily shouting "mush" while you amble across the tundra, enjoying the picturesque Canadian scenery, perhaps sipping from a warm mug of hot chocolate as you go. Clinging is more the name of the game, plus quite a lot of shouting and swearing as pine trees, rocks and cliff edges swerve into your vision and then out again as you flash by.

* * *

They also never stop running.

You've seen *The Terminator*, right? Well, your basic T-800 model cyborg huskies just follow the ones in front, and they keep on going at the same relentless pace for ever, until you grow old and die, still on the sled. There will still be huskies circling the planet, long after the human race has decamped for the stars, because Keeping On Going is just what huskies do.

Huskies do stop running for two reasons though. One – if the dog team in front stops, yours stops too. (I have no idea how the very front team stops. I think it must be something to do with dog biscuits.) And two – they stop when you fall off.

Note, that's when, not if.

* * *

You'll fall off. Again and again.

Think about it. You're on a low-slung slidey sled, going at a zillion miles per hour, powered by monomaniacal zombie-dogs. And frankly, you're rubbish at it; you haven't had the training. And the dogs only understand French. And you're confusing them by anglicising the one French word they actually know.

Of course you're going to fall off.

But amazingly, when you do, the dogs stop running straight away and you lie there under an upturned sled. The world comes slowly into view as you clear the snow from your eyes and nostrils, and you slowly realise that the panting you can hear is not from your expelled breath but from a line of stationary huskies, straining at their harness. You test your limbs gingerly and push yourself back up off the ground.

But hang on, whatever you do …

* * *

Don't put both feet back on the sled until you're ready. Because then the huskies just start running again, whether you're balanced on properly or not.

It's a dog thing. Sled upturned – idiot human fallen off. One foot on sled – idiot human still not ready. Two feet on – idiot human good to go.

Basically, over the course of the day, you do a lot of falling off, getting half back on again, being dragged for a while through the glorious Canadian wilderness, and then falling off again. There's lots of laughing. In French. At you.

* * *

That big open expanse you're on? That's a lake.

Suddenly you can see for miles. All the trees have disappeared, and Canada opens up in front of you in all its white-snow, blue-sky glory. It's majestic, and even the huskies seem to be enjoying the view.

Hang on. No trees. That's because you're in the middle of a huge lake. A frozen lake, about half a mile deep. They don't tell you that before you set off. They don't ask if you'd rather go around Icy-Water-of-Doom Lake, they just run right across it.

* * *

One more thing. How shall I put this? Huskies are very busy, what with the running and all. They don't have time for bathroom breaks, so they just go – and I'm talking both Watering the Tundra and Dropping a Husky Bomb – on the go, if you see what I mean.

Now the sled is behind the huskies, and you're being pulled along at great speed in their wake. Do the maths.

I think we'll leave it there. Try to keep your mouth closed, would be my advice. Yellow snow is very definitely a thing.

* * *

Huskies are amazing and Canada is truly beautiful. And while, to be fair, we knew these two things already (mainly because everyone in Canada tells you these two things), you don't necessarily get to appreciate them at the time.

But after a couple of hours – when you realise that you haven't fallen off for a bit, and that you didn't plummet through the lake ice and, hello, was that an actual moose? – both huskies and Canada come together in glorious symbiosis. It's blindingly obvious that this is an excellent way to see this extraordinary country, and you begin to muse on the possibility of getting your own husky team, just for weekends, or maybe even to take you to work, and after all, they're hardly any trouble …

Then you fall off again.

***

This was an extract from Don't Eat the Puffin: Tales From a Travel Writer's Life by Jules Brown

Find Out More

IF YOU ENJOYED this book, here's how to find out more about upcoming books, projects, trips and events.

Join in at Jules Told Me!

I blog about travel and travel-writing at julestoldme.com, where there are features on over 30 countries, plus posts about life as a travel writer and how to self-publish. I also make quirky travel videos on my YouTube channel – why not drop by and say hi!

Books by Trust-Me Travel

Trust-Me Travel is the name of my book publishing company. I write and publish travel memoirs, travel guides with a twist and how-to guides for travel writers. I'm always happy to consider offers, suggestions and ideas for new books, projects or collaborations.

Connect with Jules

Facebook: @JulesBrownWriter
Twitter: @JulesBrown4
Blog: julestoldme.com

Made in the USA
Middletown, DE
01 May 2023

29796234R00116